The 21st Century Parent

Parent

*Multicultural Parent Engagement
Leadership Strategies Handbook*

The 21st Century Parent

Multicultural Parent Engagement Leadership Strategies Handbook

Mary Johnson

Parent-U-Turn

INFORMATION AGE PUBLISHING, INC.
Charlotte, NC • www.infoagepub.com

Library of Congress Cataloging-in-Publication Data

Johnson, Mary.
 The 21st century parent : multicultural parent engagement leadership
strategies handbook / Mary Johnson.
    p. cm.
 Includes bibliographical references.
 ISBN 978-1-61735-853-1 (pbk.) – ISBN 978-1-61735-854-8 (hardcover) –
ISBN 978-1-61735-855-5 (ebook) 1. Education–Parent
participation–California–Los Angeles–Handbooks, manuals, etc. 2. School
improvement programs–California–Los Angeles. 3.
Multiculturalism–California–Los Angeles. 4. Parent-U-Turn (Organization)
I. Title.
 LB1048.5.J67 2012
 371.19'2–dc23

                                                                      2012016432

Copyright © 2012 Information Age Publishing Inc.

Printed in the United States of America

In Loving Memory and in Honor of

Emma Louise Hardwick Street

*Parent, Grandparent, Friend, Parent Organizer, Education
Researcher, and Advocate for Equality*

1939–2009

Contents

Introduction

An informed parent is a powerful instrument for social change.
—Mary Johnson

Getting Started

The 21st Century Parent: A Handbook for Urban Parents and Educators offers an authentic model for powerful parent involvement in urban schools.

Single Mother on Welfare to Education Activist

After being married for 20 years and more, I found myself a single mother on welfare. I was a welfare single mother raising four children. I always thought that marriage was forever, but my husband had other ideas. This wasn't a hand that I would have dealt for myself. It wasn't easy raising three sons and one daughter. I was determined that my children weren't going to be the victims of divorce. They never asked to be born, and why should they have less because of adult issues. Some days we had Top Ramen and hot dogs, but our stomachs were full. I knew that the only way out for my children was a good education. I have a high school education and some college, but I was a stay-at-home mom. I believed that a mother should be with her children and bond with them from birth to 5 years old. There is an 8 year difference between my oldest son and my next son. Between that time, I worked outside the home. I always worked at jobs that had me home when my children got out of school. My husband was going through his midlife crisis, and I didn't have time to run after him and lose focus on my children. My husband moved out and left us to survive on our own. That meant no money, and I was forced to go on welfare.

The choice of being on welfare was my last choice, but it was the only choice or hungry and homeless for me and my children. I was never a quitter, and I was of good stock and strong will. Many nights, I didn't sleep as I worried about paying rent. I soon realized that I must stop feeling sorry for myself and take control of my own journey. I realized there was money to be made within my 350-apartment complex. There were many people in the same situation that I was in who couldn't pay their rent. So I decided to go to the Crown Bookstore. I bought all the self-help books on how to do eviction and bankruptcy. After reading the books, I started posting fliers in every apartment unit's laundry room. To my surprise, I didn't have to wait too long before I got my first client. So after the first client, the word got out fast about my service. This service allowed me to put food on my table and a roof over my children. This was only a stepping stone. I wanted my children to not want for anything, like before the separation. Someone had to be the grownup and act on behalf of what is good for the children. I decided that it was time to put end to my marriage. I needed to think with my mind and not let my heart lead me. I went to the Crown Bookstore again and got a book on filing for divorce. I used the self-help book guide to fill out the form. I prepared the paperwork and filed for the divorce, but waited another 5 years before going through with it. In my heart, I was holding on to hope that my family would come back together, but it didn't. After I got the news that my husband was going to have a baby outside the marriage, I knew that was the final straw. I went back to court and divorced him. He never showed up for the court hearing, and I received everything I asked for—full custody of the children, alimony, and child support. I left the courthouse very relieved. That same day I went to my ex-husband and dropped off the wage assignment court order; now I wouldn't have to stay up worrying about if I could make rent or buy my children shoes. Every week on Tuesday, when they cut his check, they cut a check for me and my children. I'd never seen my husband cry until I took his money. The only question he had for me was "What did I do to you?" The only thing that mattered to him was his money, not his family that he left behind. It was very hard for me to let go of the past, but slowly I got to know more of how to be single again and less of being someone's wife. I started getting busy working with my children in their schools and outside activities. I believed that you can lived in a community and not be a part of it. I enrolled all my children into sports activities so they didn't have the time to hang out. My children went from school to home, doing homework then to the park.

Yes, my schedule was busy, but that is a sacrifice we as mothers make for our children. I would drop all four children at different locations, dividinge my time so I could spend time at each child's event. Yet it was frustrating, but the smiles you get when your child looks up and sees you there makes it all worth it. I even started to coach my children, and I was happy just as much as the children were. Many of the things that I was doing, such as coaching and volunteering at school, I probably wouldn't have experienced if I was still married. I many ways, I was old fashioned; I'd thought the mother role was inside the home. Many of my friends were watching out for job openings for me, and the first job offer was driving public buses. I didn't stay long because of the hours; I would leave my home at 4:30a.m. and return at 5 p.m. I never wanted my children to be latchkey kids. Even though the pay was great, my children were more valuable than the money. I left that job, and then I applied at a temporary agency. To my surprise, they had jobs available at a hospital only 2 miles from my home. This new job had hours closer to those of the school day and the same holidays off that aligned the with the school calendar. It wasn't the ideal job schedule, but it would do for now.

The extra money from the job allowed me to take my sons and daughter to movies, Disneyland, Knott's Berry Farm, and do things working class parents couldn't afford. After 2 years of working at the hospital, I got laid off. So, back to drawing board again to find the ideal job. After being laid off for a couple of months, a friend told me about a job at the school district. My friend went to her boss and spoke to him about me. Two days after, I went to interview at the school district. My interview was about who I was and about my Christian beliefs. I was never asked any questions about my skills. I got the job, and now I was truly happy because now I could leave the house at the same time and return home at same time my children arrived. We finally were on the same schedule, and I would be home to greet my children after a day of school. Even though the children had only one parent living in the home, I wanted them to know that they were loved. I lived my life for my children, which meant no dating, because I thought that would come between me and my children. I didn't want my children to feel that they had to share me with anyone. Even though they are all grown up, we are still close as ever. Some of my children live outside California and the United States, but we speak with each other at least four times a day.

Key Factors:
Self-advocate, self-preparation, self-preservation

Special Education Advocacy

I started as an advocate for my son and daughter. It wasn't very easy, because I had no knowledge about the process or if my children had special needs. I thought that my kids were struggling with classroom assignments. The first time that I realized that my son had a serious problem was when he was in the 4th grade. He had a teacher who didn't want to be in an inner city school. She would tell her students in the classroom that they couldn't have a party at Halloween or Christmas like the other students. The reason was that her students were smart enough, and they didn't have the time to waste. One day, my son came home in tears; he felt different than the other students at school. I told my son not to worry about what the teacher said; that he was just as normal as everyone else was. I explained to my son that if he lived in another part of the world that read from left to right, then he would be the normal one, and they would be the ones with a disability. I then explained to my son that if you tie your shoes, think for yourself, dress and feed yourself, you aren't disabled. This only means that he is unique and that a person must teach him how he learns, not how they want to teach. The next day I went to the school and met with the principal. In that meeting, I requested that my son be removed from his current teacher. I was outraged and angry; "no" was not an option that I wanted to hear from principals. After speaking with the principal regarding my belief that the teacher was killing my son's spirit, and confidence in myself, the principal agreed to remove my son to another teacher. A week later I requested an Individual Evaluation Process (IEP) for my son. In the meantime, I went to the Crown Bookstore again and bought many book on the topic of student rights regarding special education. I wanted to prepare myself for a meeting. It was amazing how my son's spirit of learning returned after removing him from his previous classroom. That same year, my son earned the Most Improved Student award. The light bulb came on; I knew I must play major roles in the pathway of my son's education. I got an IEP in 50 days after I requested the meeting. I was scared and uncomfortable. What helped me the most was that I believed that I was my son's first teacher. In the IEP, an administrator spoke of a special dayschool for my son, but that wasn't going to happen on my watch. The self-help book on special education had prepared me well; I knew my son had the right to be taught with his peers in a mainstream classroom. After I told the committee that I wouldn't sign the IEP, they soon moved to another topic. Even though I didn't know everything about special education, the school staff thought I did.

Key Factors:
Learning school structure, investigate your rights, know or have knowledge of laws that protect both your rights and your child's rights.

UCLA Parent Center X

The UCLA Parent Project probably was a life saver for me and many other parents in Lynwood. What I remember most about the UCLA Parent Project was Dr. Angela Hasan. Dr Hasan was from UCLA, but she was different in the things that came out of her mouth. She actually believed in parents as equal partners; it wasn't just words, she put it into action. Many times she stood side-by-side on hot issues on how to involve parents. I am an employee of Lynwood Unified School District (LUSD), and Dr. Hasan asked me to recruit parents for her project. I went back to my school, Hosler Middle, and set up a table on back-to-school night and recruited 40 parents. One of the parents that I recruited was Emma Street. She was walking by, and I tried to stop her, and her response was, "I will be back." I told myself she's not coming back. To my surprise, she came back, and I signed her up. The next day, she came back and told me that she couldn't attend the first meeting because of medical reasons. I volunteered to go to meeting in her place—to hold her spot. She agreed, and from that day on she was my right hand in working with the UCLA Parent Project in Lynwood. The UCLA Parent Project changed the way parents participated at Lynwood Unified Schools. The parents' traditional roles were bathroom and hall monitors and PTA. None of these activities had ever increased student achievement in the classroom.

The UCLA Parent Project was focused on student achievement in the classroom. We as parents were learning about what was needed to improve student achievement in the classroom. The UCLA Parent Project was a 13-week series of workshops. The parents attended one workshop a week for 3 hours. The parents were put into the same learning environment that children attended school in. This meant that the parents were exposed to math, literacy, science, college-going culture, and special education. It was so amazing to see parents learning how to do math and science who had very little knowledge in those topics. For example, Emma Street, a 65-year-old great-grandmother who was raising her grandchildren and great-grandchildren, learned how to do algebra by using beans from the kitchen. She learned how to use an item that she uses every day to apply to her learning. She was so proud that day that she learned something new, and now she could pass that knowledge on to her grandchildren. Before the UCLA Parent Project, parents visiting the classroom were limited to the observation of their children, but with the project, we were able to visit the classroom to observe classroom activities. We learned how to observe a classroom, such as what to look for on bulletin boards, the seating patterns of students, and teacher engagement with the students overall or with the blackboard. After 13 weeks of training, parents graduated at UCLA. This was done because the majority of parents hadn't graduated from schools or had no positive experience with schools. The parents were allowed to bring their family to the graduation dinner. For many it was the first time anyone from their family had graduated from a university. After the project, these same parents advanced to being facilitors at their school. This was the first time that parents were put in leadership positions of which they were directors. What UCLA did was to train the parents to do professional development and support with resources to re-create the project themselves. In many cases this was the first time parents ever held down a paid position. I believe UCLA came into Lynwood with the purpose of training parents to "fish," thus providing them with a skill for a lifetime. I gave Dr. Hasan many kudos for remembering her roots in the 'hood, and realizing that parents who have knowledge are powerful for school reform.

Key Factors:
Learning the laws that govern the school structure in pre-K–12 grades helps you navigate your child beyond high school into college.

American Education Research Association

I am very honored to be able to have presented at the American Educational Research Association. I love to attend AERA because it gives me a Parent Researcher/Practitioner space and opportunity to share my data with scholars. I don't relate to many terms that are used to describe low-income people. It seems that we are in two different worlds. For example, I attended a workshop with scholars and a Los Angeles Unified School District (LAUSD) superintendent. The superintendent was from local District 7. They were speaking on how great everything was going in District 7. All of this was lies; this district had the lowest-performaning schools. Yes, they spent a lot of money for consultants from higher education, but that made very little difference for student achievement. Since we were in the audience, the presenters had to change their strategies and data. Myself and other Los Angeles Unified School parents twho were present challenged the findings.

The superintendent suspended her presentation and started to share the true facts about the district. What I noticed was that scholars don't challenge or are critical of their peers' works. They are too busy clapping each other on the back—it's just a vacation for them—but sadly their work and findings are used to stereotype us in the inner cities. Somehow they feel that because you are poor that something is wrong with your brain. Most of the blame on failure in inner cities is on poverty, not the conditions or who is teaching our children. Instead, the scholars seem to be dazzled by graphics and charts; they really need to put a face on their work, and just maybe they might get it right. Other parent leaders and I realized that until the scholars leave the universities and come among the people that they write about, their conferences will only be a vacation away from university. Even for those parent researchers who attended the last seven conferences with others parents, there is no accounting for us like there are for interns and students. Maybe parents as researchers are best kept secret.

Key Factors:
Parents are now doing research on conditions and barriers within urban communities and now are presenting our data to university scholars. We realize that the true experts on solutions for inner cities or rural communities come from people within.

Working With the State Assembly Office Regarding Parent Violation

The meeting with state assemblyman Marco Fireburgh was to resolve Lynwood parent conflicts with the LUSD regarding parent involvement. The Lynwood Unified School District had very little respect for parents and being in compliance with the No Child Left Behind (NCLB) Act of 2001. The school district was treating parents like they had no rights or voice. Some of the schools were appointing parents to school councils without an election. Plus, they were spending money with no input or suggestions from parents. All of this was a violation of the California Education Codes and NCLB Section 1118. So I organized a group of parents, and we filled out a Uniform Complaint Procedures (UCP) form regarding category funds. Before we filled out the UCP form, we met with Federal and State Compliance officers and superintendents, but no one would listen. After all doors were closed in my face, it was time to take action. We went as far as to get articles in local newspapers saying that the Lynwood Unified School District had

Left Parents Behind. We knew this wasn't going to be another victory, so we reached out to our assemblyman Marco Fireburgh.

Marco Fireburgh was the speaker of the house. I called my assemblyman for an appointment. While waiting for the appointment, we parents wrote down all the violations and the laws that were broken. Eventually we got an appointment with the assemblyman. Our next step was to ensure that we captured all the violations and aligned them with the laws. In a couple of days, I got a call from the Assemblyman Office manager with an appointment date. My next step was ensuring that all the right individuals would be at the table for the meeting. I wanted to ensure fairness, so I invited members of the Institute for Democracy, Education, and Access (IDEA) from UCLA. I chose Dr. John Rogers because he had mentored us on the laws that govern education. The day of the meeting, seven parent leaders and I joined the assemblyman and Lynwood Unified School District board members and State and Federal Compliance Officers. The assemblyman was there to mediate the meeting. I presented to the LUSD representatives our list of 40 violations aligned with NCLB. We went down the list one complaint at a time. Each complaint was acted on separately so we could agree on whether it was a violation or not. Out of the 40 violations, we all came to agreement on 34 as being out of compliance. The next step was for LUSD board members and Compliance Officers to go back to the LUSD and present our findings. They voted to accept the findings and signed a Memorandum of Understanding with us to oversee the parent involvement in the LUSD. The agreement allowed us to stop category funds when there was violation regarding excluding parent participation. The LUSD sent out a memo to all principals and school sites regarding our roles and the schools' responsibility to be in compliance. Parents are now included in the hiring interview process for teachers and principals, strategy planning, and the yearly LUSD parent-needs assessment.

Key Factors:

The parents challenged the school structure and won after appealing to the State of California. We attained a resolution against the Lynwood Unified School District for 34 violations. We are now the outside evaluators for parent engagement over a Local Education Agency.

We used all resources such as media, university professors, and local politicians.

Southwood Apartment Conflict With the South Gate Police Department

Southwood Apartments was a complex with about 350 apartment units. We nicknamed the complex "Pendleton Ave." This was a large complex but not a housing project, because the rent was cheap, but there was much similarity. There was much crime activity and very little police protection. Plus, we had very little respect for policemen. The crime wasn't against the people who lived in the complex but against anyone who came into the complex. The ice cream truck and pizza man dared not go through the private gate. We would have to meet the pizza man outside the gate because he would get robbed of his pizza and money. Yet everyone in complex felt safe; within the gate, it was home. One day the police department came with portal police station to harsh residents. They were knocking on everyone's doors, asking who lived there. When they came to my door, I refused to tell them who lived in my apartment. I started to ask questions such as what was this information going to be used for. They soon realized that I wasn't going to share any information; they then moved on. I followed them down the steps of the apartment to observe their activities. They were pulling people out of their apartments. It was like a movie about Nazi Germany. I have never seen anything like this; only in the movies. Everyone in the complex started to come out of their apartments just to watch. My neighbor went and got her camcorder and started to record the police action.

When the policeman saw her, he started to walk forward toward her and she ran. She hid her camcorder under my barbeque pit outside my door. The police found the camcorder and knock on my door. My 8-year-old daughter answered the door, and police asked her who the camcorder belonged to, and she thought he was speaking of the barbeque pit. My daughter responded to police officer that it was ours. I heard the police at my door, and I returned back to my apartment. The police officer told me that the camcorder was stolen and that they were going to take my daughter down to the station. I became very emotional—not my baby! I asked to speak to his supervisor and he told me, "You don't want to speak to him. He's worse than me." By then my tears had turn to outrage. So I told him to take her in and I would meet him at the station; and since she was a juvenile, she would be back home in an hour. The more the police officer spoke, the more I insisted that he take her down to the station and book her.

The officer realized that I no longer was going to be bullied by him, so he told me he was going to take the camcorder and run a check against stolen property. After all the police officers left the complex, I received a call from the Watch Commander. My neighbor went down to the police station to claim her camcorder. I explained to my neighbor that she didn't break any laws; she was filming the complex. Early the next morning, I called my friend Dora Long and she went door-to-door with a petition against the Police Department activity. The petition explained to residents that the Police Department had overstepped their boundaries and instead of "Protect and Serve," they violated our rights. We got 750 signatures on the petition. We waited for the next City Hall meeting to present our petition. I wanted to send a message to the council and Police Department, so I told 35 residents about meeting. This would be my first time ever attending a City Council meeting.

While waiting for the meeting to start, a friend came up to me and asked me what I was doing there. I began to tell him what happened at the apartment complex. After I explained our incident, he brought to us a gentleman named George Troxcil. He was the Police Chief. He asked me not to present the petition to the council, and he would get back to me first thing in morning. There was something about him that convinced me that he was a man of his word. He called the next morning, and I met his Sergeant and his Captain. At first, this was a hostile meeting; the Sergeant and I looked at each other and rolled our eyes. We soon got beyond those feelings and started to work collaborativly to build relations between the Police Department and the complex.

The partnership built respect for each other. The Police Department started to hold meetings inside the complex regarding issues of concern. With the help of the Police Department, we were able to force the apartment owner to bring all apartments up to housing standards. Plus, they supported our petition to the landlord to put a playground in the complex. We residents soon realized that we could and should help the Police Department get rid of the criminal activities that had plagued the complex. After 10 years, the complex is still free from criminal activities, and the relationship with the Police Department continues.

Key Factors:
Standing up for human rights, challenge unfair practices, document concerns, speak out at public meetings.

South Gate High School Peaceful Walk-Outs

After 25 years of lobbying and protesting for a traditional school calendar of 180 days at South Gate High, the principal and school council did all they could do to get the school ready for the successful opening of a new school year. I don't think that the Los Angeles Unified School District was happy, because without Track School Concept 6, which governed the school calendar, a lot of funding and grants would be lost. At that time, I was president of School Site Council and Title 1 council. We did all we could do by going to roadshows and ordering books in March. It seemed that the district dropped the ball. I remember like it was yesterday. I was in the Parent Center on the second flo of their classes.

When the parents went running down the steps to the ground floor, all the students were in the lunch area—about 500 students. The students were sitting on the ground in a peaceful manner. After the bell rang, the students started to walk to the football field to the bleachers. The principal and staff all went out to the football field followed by parents. The students refused to talk to the principal and school staff. They asked for me to mediate their concerns. The concerns of students were that they didn't have permanent teachers in core classes and no books. The majority of students who walked out of class were Gate and Honor students. The majority of the students had a D to F average. Plus, this was South Gate High's first year on the quarter system. The first thing I did was to ask the parents to collect money among them and get bottled water for the students. Then I told the students that I would come back every 20 minutes to update them on discussions. They had to promise me that they would stay peaceful. While I was speaking with the students, a Los Angeles Unified School District downtown administrator grabbed the microphone out of my hand.

The students became out outraged and started to shout to give me the mic. Suddenly another parent grabbed the mic from the administrator and gave it back to me. The principal made it clear to everyone that I was a part of his team. I was able to negotiate that no students would be punished for walking out and that all students would be able to keep the grades they earned or drop the grades and make up that grade in the next quarter. The principal agreed that he would meet with different groups on the campus, because he now realized that the student body didn't always reflect all the students' thinking. It was great to see the students advocating for themselves and allow me to be a part of their movement. Every parent leader that was there was so proud of our children that day; they'd walked out but stayed inside the school to protest in a peaceful rally.

▬▬▬▬▬▬

Key Factors:
Peace rally, teamwork, student's self-advocacy, organizing by parents and students, resolution of conflict.

Stanford Elementary Parents Stop School Budget

I was a member of School Site and Title 1 for Stanford Avenue Elementary School. Sometimes it was very hard to go to meetings because there was no collaboration or teamwork. The teachers would be on one side and the parents the other, and the principal looking for allies. There were lines drawn before you got into the meeting room. We the parents already knew how to vote on all the items on the agenda. There was one teacher who we could count on to vote with the parents. This would give us an advantage. The problem was that we had a coordinator who didn't respect the parents. The coordinator would be meeting to hear the teachers' input and suggestions, but never reach out to the parents. He would present to us the teachers' suggestions or ideas.

The law states that we are supposed to engage in the initial process. There was a committee made by the principal and coordinator that excluded parents as participants. I filed a UCP form complaining that the school had excluded parents as equal partners as per No Child Left Behind Section 1118. I got 50 parents to sign the UCP form with me. This made it stronger than if just one individual complained. We appealed our complaint to the State of California Education Department. We won our complaint and the LAUSD met with us and asked what we wanted. The district explained that the money was frozen and that they would have to lay off individuals if we didn't come to an agreement. My response to the school district was that we just wanted them to do the right process to include us and our voices as equal partners in the budget process. We the parents agreed to an emergency meeting that was a day long, and we came up with a balanced budget that included all stakeholders.

Key Factors:

Bring transparency, accountability, compliance to laws; every voice and input matters; parents are equal partners in school decision making.

South Gate Middle School Attempts to Turn South Gate High School Into a Magnet School

Several years ago, there was a group of South Gate ladies who wanted to turn South Gate High School into magnet school. I was in my second year as school site council. It took several years for the new principal to change the culture of the school. In the past, the culture was that Gate and Honor students were the only ones expected to go college. It would be hard to go back to that kind of backward thinking. I was very happy that my principal and union chairperson felt the same way that I did. I wasn't against magnet schools if the whole school was going to be a magnet. It was not fair to have two a tiered school. This is where some students think they are privileged or they get more opportunity than others. As soon as I heard of this, I made fliers for back-to-school night. On back-to-school night, I put a table outside the gym so I could hand out the fliers to parents.

The news of what I was doing got back to the middle school parents; right away they started to organize against me. My attitude was "bring it on." The South Gate Middle School organized a meeting for which about 900 parents showed up. No one expected me to show up, but I did. I felt 900 knives in my back. The superintendent and LAUSD members were all down front. So I went to the front and the superintendent and staff greeted me with hugs and kisses. The room went quiet—you could hear a pin drop. I never planned to stay; I just wanted them to know that I could not be intimidated. After 5 minutes of chatting with district folk, I left and went home. I wanted to let the superintendent know that I was watching and that I wasn't going away. I did some investigation and found out the school couldn't be turned into a magnet if the principal was against it. The superintendent called a meeting with middle school parents and offered another school in South Gate; the parents turned him down because the school was too close to Jordan High, a Black school. The superintendent told them to take it or leave it. The parents knew that the superintendent wasn't going to change his mind, so they accepted his offer for Southeast High School.

Key Factors:
All students should have the same opportunity and experience for a quality education; there should not be two-tiered schools, where you have and have not.

Appling for Public School Choice in the LAUSD

In recent years, the Los Angeles Unified School District and the State of California have been wondering what to do with the lowest-performing schools. So the LAUSD came up with the idea of giving away the publically funded schools to a charter agency. The district actually gave away a brand new school, not the older school that was in need of repair. When you hear the words "public school choice," you think that the public has a choice. If you thought that, you would be wrong, because the choice was limited to hand-picked groups of parents who were connected to some of the board members who were promoting the resolution. As the chairperson of Parent Collaborative, I was outraged that my district parent council was excluded from advisory votes on this issue. The Parent Collaborative council represented all 700,000 parents in the LAUSD. I informed my committee that we must take action because the district was not transparent in their action and they had disrespected the parents of the LAUSD and only worked with outside nonprofit parents. This was a violation of NCLB Section 1118. What bothered me the most was that it was my board member, who represents the schools in my community, who was the author of the resolution. Plus, in the past, the president of board and my board member had worked with me on successful projects, and this time, for some strange reason, they chose not to.

So I organized my parents for an upcoming meeting when the item of public school choice would be on the agenda. I went out and bought T-shirts so we would be sending a message. The message was that the Los Angeles Unified Board has excluded the voices of the students whom they serve. The boardroom was full with all the stakeholders, from the teacher's union, parent leaders, and nonprofit groups. When I got up to speak, all 50 of my members stood beside in support of our stand against the district policy. I wasn't against the policy, but how it was done: hand picking only individuals who agreed with their vision. To many it seemed that this resolution was a backdoor agreement in the middle of the night—it lack transparency. Even though the item passed, my board member who was the author of the resolution contacted me immediately and asked if she could set up weekly meetings with me and my executive board members. I believe the reason that she contacted me was because my speech wasn't an attack on the resolution, but it was more about transparency and how we had successfully worked together in past. Our first meeting with the board member was a little heated, but as chairperson, I ensured that every member acted professionally. Even though we weren't included in the initial process from that period, the district included the Parent Collaborative but not the District Advisory Council, which represented all Title 1 schools. Even though we met with the board member, it didn't change our minds about public school choices.

I personally had to make a choice because one public school choice was bidding on a new school in my neighborhood. I am not very fond of charter schools because the data isn't in yet and it is not a magic bullet. Another reason is that charter schools don't have to play by same rules as public schools; they are able to get waivers from the district or state. I am a firm believer that something must be done to public schools to guarantee quality education to all children, regardless of income, barriers, or the condition of the neighborhood. What I didn't like about the process was that, even though all stakeholders were supposed to have a hand in the writing process, the teachers wrote the plan and then presented it to the parents. It was the same old status quo plan. So I decided to challenge the teacher plan. I wanted a plan in which parents would have a voice in the initial processes and not after the fact. I knew that I must surround myself and parents with experts who were open and wanted to make a difference in children's lives.

This was our time to put something forward outside the traditional classroom environment. I couldn't have done this without the support of Dr. Geni Boyer, who believed in parents and their right to play major roles in school reform. We immediately went to work on forming our team. The first thing I did was to write a list of connected resources and individuals that could be used for the benefit of submitting a successful plan to the LAUSD. I remember we wanted to be transparent and available to the public, so we held our meeting at the Sizzler restaurant, where everyone was welcome. It was very nice that Sizzler allowed us to use their banquet room as a meeting place. We chose a principal who was very successful in opening a school in which all students were achieving. Plus, she grew up in a similar community and believed that all children can learn, and she embraced parents as equal partners. We traveled through the community, introducing our plan and how it was different from the charter and teacher plans.

It wasn't easy because I was being attacked by some teachers who claimed that I didn't live in South Gate because I was Black. There was a report that I was from David Brewer, the ex-superintendent that was let go and replaced. There were some parent leaders who questioned, "What has Mary Johnson ever done for this community?" Still, the attacks didn't stop me from doing what I believed was right for all the children of South Gate. I went out and partnershiped with the Pearson book company, UCLA, and Pepperdine University. In public school choice, there is a voting process; and the community came out to vote. I knew that I didn't have money like the charter and teacher's union, but I had people power. In community votes, my plan took second behind the teachers union's plan. There was a peer review of the plan, and my plan did well. So I named the proposed school Urban Prep Academy. My intentioin was for the school to provide an alternative to South Gate, where child accountability, flexibility, innovation, parent choice, parent-teacher involvement, and public-private partnerships could combine to provide a better future for students.

The new school will be an international school open to *all* students—irrespective of gender, ethnicity, or national origin—who seek an international education in a multilingual setting based on the International Baccalaureate Primary Years Program. We wanted to bring in a school that would prepare students in elementary with a college-going culture.

Student Outcomes

Students who participate in Urban Prep's educational program will strive to have and to exhibit the attributes of an "educated person" in the 21st century.

Urban Preparatory Academy learners will strive to be

- Inquirers: They develop their natural curiosity and acquire the skills necessary to conduct inquiry and research and show independence in learning. They actively enjoy learning, and this love of learning will be sustained throughout their lives.
- Knowledgeable: They explore concepts, ideas, and issues that have local and global significance. In so doing, they acquire in-depth knowledge and develop understanding across a broad and balanced range of disciplines.
- Thinkers: They exercise initiative in applying thinking skills critically and creatively to recognize and approach complex problems and make reasoned, ethical decisions.
- Communicators: They understand and express ideas and information confidently and creatively in more than one language and in a variety of modes of communication. They work effectively and willingly in collaboration with others.
- Principled: They act with integrity and honesty, with a strong sense of fairness, justice, and respect for the dignity of the individual, group, and community. They take responsibility for their own actions and accept the consequences that accompany them.
- Open-Minded: They understand and appreciate their own cultures and personal histories, and are open to the perspectives, values, and traditions of other individuals and communities. They are accustomed to seeking and evaluating a range of points of view and are willing to grow from the experience.
- Caring: They show empathy, compassion, and respect toward the needs and feelings of others. They have a personal commitment to service, and act to make a positive difference in the lives of others and for the environment.
- Risk Takers: They approach unfamiliar situations and uncertainty with courage and forethought, and have the independence of

spirit to explore new roles, ideas, and strategies. They are brave and articulate in defending their beliefs.

- Balanced: They understand the importance of intellectual, physical, and emotional balance to achieve personal well-being for themselves and others.
- Reflective: They give thoughtful consideration to their own learning and experience. They are able to assess and understand their strengths and limitations in order to support their learning and personal development.

Even though I was getting reports that the LAUSD had already made a deal with the charter agency, regardless of who voted or blessed the plan, the charter agency would be the winner. These reports were coming from district administrators. The icing on the cake was when a close friend of mine, who is a part of the Los Angeles City Mayor's group, called and invited me to lunch. At lunch, I discussed with him my proposal for one of the schools that was up for public school choice. He told me to let him make a call and speak with his connection at the school district. After hanging up the phone, he told me the bad news: the school was already given away before it was put up for bid as a charter school. Plus, I was informed that my board member was upset with me because I submitted a plan. My belief is that she was mad because at the end of the day, a group of parents submitted the best proposal. Our plan was labeled as too aggressive for our neighborhood. To me, that meant we the parents had higher expectations for our students than Los Angeles Unified Board members. What I did was give a platform for parents and the community to have a voice in the changes that were taking place in the City of South Gate.

Key Factors:
We want to make a difference in how our children are being educated in our community. We want to create a school that challenges our children as critical thinkers in early schooling with civic engagement and a dual language program. These are the skills that will help our children to be successful in the 21st-century global community and achieve the American dream.

One Parent Model Doesn't Fix All Schools

As a parent of urban children attending public schools in a community of color, the only model you hear about in Joyce Epstein and PTA, and neither one was making any major difference in our schools. Students of color have the highest dropout rate, lowest academic performance, lowest high school graduation rate, and the highest rate of students who enter prison. I give all due respect to Dr. Joyce Epstein for being the pioneer for parent involvement; but I truly believe that in the 21st century, we need to urge parents into action beyond mere involvement. It wasn't until I met a young lady from San Diego who shares some of my same philosophy. Many nights we stayed on the telephone talking about our concerns regarding the California Department of Education (CDE) and consultants who talk of parent involvement and lack of parent engagement in California. The only model that was embraced by the CDE was by Joyce Epstein and the PTA. So we started pressure for data and evaluation of models in schools that have an Academic Performance Index (API) of 1–5.

We wanted to know how the model had changed the outcomes for children who attended these schools. To our surprise, there was no data or case studies to support promoting a one-model system. Everyone within the Family Area Network (FAN) group seemed to be upset because they thought we were attacking Dr. Joyce Epstein; we just asked the question, "What if?" We had worked for years as parent-practitioners, and we hadn't seen any "bake sale" model to promote academic improvement in the classroom. Yes, parents engaged in limited roles in sales of baked goods or materials to raise money for Teacher-Appreciation Day, and just maybe you might get some playground equipment. After we couldn't get the data that we requested from the CDE, we decided to put up an online petition. The petition stated, "One School Model Doesn't Fix All Schools." The petition was directed at Jack O'Connell, Secretary of Education. Our survey was posted on the SurveyMonkey online network. We got over 1,000 signatures. The online survey had signatures from parent leaders and professors. The survey soon got results, most notably phones calls from California Department of Education.

The question asked was, "What do you want from us?" Our response was that we want multiply voices at the table, starting with parent practitioners, the individuals who are working in inner cities schools, and who have great success in engaging parents to action on behalf of their children. After many correspondences back and forth, there was very little movement. After seeing that we were at a brick wall, we decided to write to Jack O'Connell and Zollie Stevenson of the U.S. Department of Education. This is a sample of the e-mail letter:

> To Honorable Jack O' Connell and Dr. Zollie Stevenson,
>
> I am very disappointed to report that at this time there has been a breakdown in communication with CDE regarding One Model Doesn't Fix All Califor-

nia Schools range of API 1–3 schools. Three months ago Diane Haney and I sent Jack O' Connell five nonnegotiable. We were asked to work with CDE staffs to resolve the issues. We have been transparent and collaborative and I am disappointed to inform you that CDE and FAN Board have not been transparent or inclusive. Yes, we were able to have input and suggestions to revise proposed State Action Team, that's where it ended. State Action Team should reflect the entire student's population of California. The State Action Team members are a part of FAN Board and they exclude any parents as Directors from API 1–3 schools and list themselves as Directors. This is conflict of interest. There should have been diversity outreach to faith based organizations, parent practitioners.

It is times to build a 21st-century leadership that is like a starfish expansion of voices, and a reflection of all voices being respected. It not enough that Title1 parents give input and suggestions, it show disrespect to see some of our input emitted in the document. Per NCLB Section 1118 there should be a role for parents at each level. The State Action Team needs to be inclusive and add parents, community members and faith based Organization to Regional Directors. We are asking, for assistance from both State of California and US. Department of Education to hold all level of parent involvement accountability to engage parents and outreach in authentic meaningful ways at all level.

Although educators and school boards sometimes resist the idea, accountability is solely need in America's schools. Our students are falling behind those in others countries, yet compared to the foreign counterparts, our school remain subject to little accountability.

The 21st Century leaders can no longer sit on the side line and allow the gate keepers to make decisions for the urban community school with our children and keep us out. Enough is enough want change! We want our voice to be heard, respected and implemented in the plan for educating our children. The people on the FAN (Family Area Network) board and State Action Team don't look like the urban community. They cannot relate with the needs of the urban community. That is why it was so crucial to have urban parents as an equal partner at the table of discussing the needs of the urban children.

Without true collaboration and shared decision making with parent leaders of the urban community with children attending schools in the API 1–3 range, there can be no real change and no possible chance of closing the academic achievement gap. Without transparency there can be no accountability. With no accountability we are left with chaos.

1. In Conclusion, we need California Department of Education to acknowledge that Joyce Epstein model is JUST ONE best practice model and that the state needs to account specifically for the needs of urban parents in at least one of its models of parent engagement.

2. We want CDE's parent engagement work to be inclusive of parents and community members representing schools that are docile 1-3 and/or schools with large proportions of students of color. (This principle should apply to any body of work or any committee doing parent engagement.

After the e-mail to Jack O'Connell, we decided to attend the next California State Education Board meeting. There was an item on the agenda about parent involvement; this was our opportunity to discuss One Model Doesn't Fix All Schools. To our surprise, the board members, especially the president of the board, was open minded to bringing this back as an agenda item. Parent involvement was put on the agenda in September 2009. It was a great day for us to see this become a reality. We didn't want to celebrate too much because we'd heard all this before and nothing came of it. We went back home from Sacramento and started to lobby parents to go to the State Board meeting in September. I was unable to make the meeting in September, but many parents from Los Angeles flew up to Sacramento.

They spoke on the need for changes in how we work with parents. Parent's echoed that each school site is different and should be allowed to use different models and that the CDE should be promoting a series of best practices and work that parent practitioners are doing at the local level. On that day, the board voted that the CDE would create a Web site that promotes best practices, and that nonprofit and practitioner information would be included on the site. Truly this was now a milestone, but still we must keep watchful eyes for compliance. There are many policies, but when the public is asleep, they will continue the status quo. After the ruling, the CDE and FAN formed a California Action Team partnership that included all the stakeholders to develop a mapping of best practices. My model was a part of the State Action Team Partnership. However, there was little movement on this model because of changes in the State Education Board membership—most of all Jack O'Connell who pushed everyone to think outside the box for the sake of all children.

Key Factors

There is no research that shows that there is any one model that has decreased dropout rates or improved student achievement. This is the main reason that the state needs to be in the business of promoting all practices and allowing the local school community to be the one that decides what fixes their schools.

Volunteer and Bring Resources to Local School Sites.

Paying forward and giving back to my community is very important to me because I believe that we are our brother's and sister's keeper. I seem to adopt several schools in my community, such as South Gate High, South Middle School, and Stanford Avenue Elementary. I usually spend 30 to 40 hours a week assisting the school in many roles, such as president of the school council, parent educator, and advocate for students. My work at local schools has earned me the respect of the principals and teachers. Many times the teachers come to me for assistance with a problem instead of going to their union. When I am missing in action, I am told by staff, "Please don't go away because it is not the same environment when you are not present." Everyone in the community thinks that I work for the school district because they see me so much.

I am always looking for extra programs that would help my schools to increase academic achievement in the classroom. One program that I reach out to is the United Way. The United Way funded a program for 4 years. The program allows mentor-teachers from Pepperdine and UCLA to go inside the classroom and work with students who are below or far below in English and math. This allows us to prepare the students for the California State Test and Exit Exam. This invention helped to improve our API and AYP (Adequate Yearly Progress) scores in last 3 years. From the elementary schools, I reached out to Pepperdine University because I believe that the dream of college is built in elementary school.

We started a college academy project for parents to share strategies on what they need to do now to lay the foundation for the future. Some of the strategy tips were very simple: take their child to visit different colleges, visit a college library, and sports activities. Our children must see themselves as belonging on college campuses, and their first exposure is in high school. I feel that middle school parents are the step-child in education. This is where children get lost in the system, so I brought the UCLA Parent Project to South Gate Middle. I wanted to engage the parents back into action. For some reason, parents seem to let go of their children after they graduate from elementary school. In my opinion, the child needs them even more. The UCLA Parent Project would lay the foundation for parents to become advocates for their children.

Key Factors:

This allows schools to have resources that schools need without coming from of their budget. These resources are directly used for the classroom and target student achievement. Getting free resources allows the schools to not have to decide between material or intervention and prevention for students.

Movement to Save Preschools

The LAUSD wanted to get rid of preschool because of budget cuts. The first and last option for cutting programs is always on the backs of children. My grandson was enrolling in preschool, and I knew the importance of preparation for kindergarten. One of the local teachers spoke to me asking what can we do to stop the district. I told her that we needed to organize the parents and educate them about the importance of preschool. I went early before school and then after school to speak with the parents about supporting the movement. After several days, I distributed fliers to the school community and handed out petition forms for parents and the community to sign.

The next step was to meet with all preschool teachers who would be losing their jobs. One of the teachers at school sent e-mails to all preschool teachers, and they came. In the meeting, we discussed the importance for everyone to go back to their school site and spread the word to parents by passing out fliers and petitions. Some of teachers weren't allowed to because their principals refused to let them participate. This didn't stop us. We continued to go to different school Parent Centers to meet with parents. Also, I called the media and got them to come out and interview the parents and students at a school. Our next move was to set a date to go to a LAUSD board meeting. We decided to take our preschoolers with us. We got two buses to take parents and students to the board meeting. We got there early to ensure that we would get into the small meeting room. Our children wore t-shirts that had the slogan "Save SLRDP Preschool," and parents had made a homemade sign. Once in the meeting room, we had all speakers sign in for public speaking comments. This would guarantee them 30–45 minutes to speak on those items.

We had to wait until 5p.m. before we got to speak to board members. I think they thought we and the children would get frustrated and go home, but they were wrong; we were committed to this event. Meanwhile, we the parents shared apples and chips with all the children. The children were getting hungry but were little soldiers that day. They too came prepare to stand in the gap for the next generation of preschoolers. I was so proud of them. There were about 75 parents and 50 preschoolers who left at 5p.m., and other parents who drove left early to pick up their other children at school. There were many excuses from the teachers union about why they had dropped preschool. They wanted to talk about an adult agenda, and we were there to talk about the children. During public comments, per Board policy, the board members aren't supposed to respond to the public, but every board member commended and dialogued with us. We told the board that we would return. I don't think they knew how soon. We returned at the next board meeting.

This time, I came with preschool teachers and past successful students from preschools who were attending college. I wanted to keep the pressure on them and keep the movement in front of people. This would affect 18,000 preschoolers next year. It seems that board members and the superintendent were upset about the teachers coming to the board meeting instead of going to work. You see, the board meeting is during the hours when many stakeholders are at work. Upon arriving back at our home school sites, the principals were waiting for the teachers that attended the board meeting in support of the parents. Every teacher that attend the board meeting with the parents and students were written up for their action. I was told that a call came from the superintendent's office. Afterwards, there was a memo to every school saying that preschool would be saved. I think they realized that we weren't going to give up and that the movement was expanding, and that it was a fight that we were committed to until the end.

Key Factors
Collaboration, teamwork, organization, recruitment, using media, dialogue with parents and teachers across Los Angeles Unified School community

This book is designed to equip parents to advocate effectively for their children and provide instructions on how parents can teach other parents these skills. Parent practitioners who practice the seven advocacy standards outlined in this book will be better able to successfully navigate their children through low-performing urban schools and into higher education.

Urban parents are often blamed for low performance and achievement. But many other factors contribute to lower performance in urban schools. The idea that inner-city parents don't care about their children is a destructive myth. Extensive research has shown the opposite—low-income urban parents actually care more about education than higher income suburban parents. But schools and teachers generally don't know how to harness the deep commitment to student success this represents. Rather than placing blame, this handbook seeks to empower parents to work alongside educators and policymakers in order to bring more equality to schools. As education adapts to the needs of the 21st century, urban parents must take on broader roles in their children's education. The need for authentic parent involvement in urban schools is increasing and will continue to increase.

Using this model of parent involvement can help urban parents participate powerfully in improving schools. This model of parent involvement promises to transform parent participation, increase student achievement, and decrease dropout rates.

About Parent-U-Turn

Parent-U-Turn (PUT) is a multicultural organization made up of an estimated 200 parents from southeast Los Angeles County and its surrounding cities. The parents of PUT have worked with UCLA researchers since 1999 to identify school conditions that have proven to be barriers to student achievement. Parent-U-Turn has been highlighted in several publications such as the *Harvard Review* (Winter edition, 2007) and *Learning Power* by Dr. Jeannie Oakes and Dr. John Rogers. In many schools, parents are taught methods and skills on how to become researchers who can help create better conditions for our children. Parent-U-Turn consists of parents, grandparents, and guardians of children in L.A. and Lynwood schools and serves multiple roles in the community, including those of politicians, activists, advocates, and teachers of many nationalities

The majority of Parent-U-Turn members range in age between 30 and 65. While these parents have no formal academic degrees, they possess a powerful amount of civic pride. Parent-U-Turn has launched many programs for school communities that seek to address how parents can best assist their schools in creating a successful learning environment. As a grassroots organization, Parent-U-Turn's leadership provides new members with opportunities to make decisions and share their voices.

The organization can best be described as a professional development program for parents. Parent-U-Turn members have a sophisticated understanding of what good teaching and learning should look like in the classroom and have struggled with some of the broader issues such as lack of textbooks, quality teachers, and parent involvement. The key issue for Parent-U-Turn members is in improving the educational opportunities of disadvantaged urban students.

Parent-U-Turn serves multiple communities in Los Angeles, but for the purpose of this book, I would like to discuss our work in the Lynwood Unified School District. Lynwood and other cities that Parent-U-Turn serves are located in the southeast area of Los Angeles County. Lynwood is 5 miles from Watts and 20 miles from Long Beach. The community of Lynwood covers a 5-mile radius and is 70% Hispanic and 30% African American, and 95% of Lynwood students receive free lunches.

Acknowledgements

I would like to thank the parents and educators who have worked endlessly to bring equality to students in urban schools. Thank you for inspiring me and ALL the support you have given me.

Parent leaders: Guadalupe Aguiar, Martha Ibarra, Justina Paque, Angelita Andrade, Leticia Guzman, Emma Street, Valerie Munoz, Jose Munoz.

Those in academia: Dr. Angela Hasan, Dr. John Rogers, Dr. Anthony Collatos, Dr. Jeff Duncan Andrade, Dr. Jeannie Oakes, Solange Belcher, Dr. Geni Boyer.

School administrators: Anna Carasco, Christopher Downing, Rita Calder, Superintendent David Brewer, Superintendent Ramon C. Cortines, Patrick Moretta, Albert Castillo, Robert Hinosjo, Dennis Boyer.

I would like to thank my family: my sons and daughter, L. C. Johnson, Ronald Johnson, Earvin Johnson, and Mya Johnson.

Most of all, I thank God.

1

The Importance of Parent Engagement

Many people write about the need to involve working class parents in education. Of course parent involvement is important, but we need to think about *how* our parents are engaged. This book describes how parents have created a distinctive approach to parent involvement—an approach that has proven powerful for parents and schools. Parents, through their inter-actions with teachers, play a major role in encouraging teachers to support learning at home. The parents of PUT have worked with UCLA researchers and local school districts in southeast Los Angeles and surrounding communities for over a decade to identify school conditions that have proven to be barriers to student achievement. This work has entailed, among other things, creating surveys, conducting focus groups, attending board meetings, holding public demonstrations, and writing news stories. All this has been done with the purpose of documenting the problematic conditions under which our children are expected to learn and their teachers are expected to work. Conversely, the ultimate goal of these endeavors is to improve those conditions in our urban schools.

The 21st Century Parent, pages 1–8
Copyright © 2012 by Information Age Publishing
All rights of reproduction in any form reserved.

The finding was that there is a high percentage of uncredentialed teachers in our neighborhoods as compared to affluent neighborhoods. Many teachers are teaching out of their subject matter. Some children have a different substitute teacher every day. The research shows that most uncredentialed teachers are teaching in low-income high-unemployment areas. This is probably the main reason that standardized test scores are lowest in neighborhoods populated by people of color. Children of color have a greater chance of being taught by uncredential teachers.

This type of action research, education work, and advocacy has required parents of color from urban communities to assume roles not traditionally expected of them. And since 1997, I have personally seen the parents I have worked with in my community find their voices, discover new identities, and reform by moving from traditional parent involvement roles to ones of greater advocacy. These are roles that parents are not used to seeing themselves in, although they are nonetheless highly capable and ready to assume them. Unfortunately, the model of many nationally recognized experts sometimes implies that working class parents of color need to be coerced or bribed, through the use of categorical state and federal programs, into participating in their children's schools or "trained" on how to be better parents and partners. As an example, many parents in Title 1 schools can get a small stipend for childcare and transportation. Many parents lie about how many children they have in order to get a check. There are parents who join committees to be able to travel to conferences outside of California. These trips are often like a vacation away from home; parents get a food voucher check, air travel, and hotel. Many times parents don't attend the conference but get a free trip. The purpose of the conference is to come back and train others parents, but this rarely happens. Many times this is the only money coming into their household. Sometimes, the principals use this to their advantage, to get the individuals who have greatest needs to be a part of committee; in many cases, they become the "rubber stampers," voting in principals' favor instead of what is good for all children.

The transformation of parents of color from school spectators to active education participants has been made possible by sharing common concerns and the collaborative conditions found in PUT. One primary difference between PUT and other organizations is that PUT is driven by the assumption that working class parents of color are more than capable of undertaking leadership roles in not only their children's schools but in their communities as well. The skills of engaging with schools are developed in PUT workshops as parent participants who may still be in the process of becoming familiar with the culture of the public school system take greater leadership roles by becoming translators, organizers, recruiters, or workshop leaders. The leadership the parents assume in PUT often transfers into the school's context, changing their form of engagement with their school. They go from being fundraisers for the Parent Teacher Association (PTA) or becoming classroom parent volunteers to members of the advisory board to the superintendent, textbook adoption committees, staff interview committees, project managers, and site coordinators for the UCLA Parent Curriculum Project Center X.

Parent-U-Turn has found that parents' overall evaluation of a teacher, their sense of comfort with the school, and their parent involvement in school activities is higher when teachers send frequent and effective communication to parents. PUT surveyed 200 teachers and parents in 2002 and 2006. Our survey targeted teachers at Lynwood High School and South Gate High School. The survey results reflected that 75% of teachers felt that parents didn't care, 65% of teachers surveyed blamed the families for children failures, and 70% of teachers reported that they lack textbooks and materials such as technology.

When communication was continual and covered both classroom content and personal information about their own child, parents were more likely to take part in school activities and events. The degree of a school administrator's enthusiasm also helped to increase parent involvement. Schools that eagerly pursued strategies to create an atmosphere of a user-friendly campus were able to engage parents in more activities than schools that excluded parent involvement.

A school administrator's enthusiasm is another factor that helps to increase parent involvement. Overall, schools that eagerly pursued the kind of strategies to create an atmosphere of a user-friendly campus that we describe in this manual were able to engage parents in more activities than schools that excluded parent involvement.

Roles for Parents in Schools Vary

Roles for parents at schools today are varied. Parent involvement efforts are effective when they allow parents the right to participate in the area in which they feel comfortable. When schools allow parents to choose which area they want to volunteer in, schools have a higher attendance level of parent involvement. Most schools measure parent involvement by attendance at parent/teacher conferences or back-to-school nights. Other types of parent engagement roles aren't respected. Many parents are comfortable volunteering as sports coaches and team moms. There are many parents who take classroom projects home and return them the same day because they have smaller children at home. These parents take projects home because small children aren't allowed in the classroom. Most schools still value only the traditional roles that parents volunteer for, such as bathroom monitors, yard supervisors, and fundraisers.

Parent-U-Turn found that when elementary school parents participated in decision making, they were motivated to increase their parent involvement. In 2004 and 2005, PUT hosted several focus groups and distributed surveys at Stanford Elementary School in the Los Angeles Unified School District (LAUSD). The survey and focus groups focused on "How to Increase Parent Involvement." There were 60 parents who participated each year in focus groups. PUT was able to distribute 100 surveys at Stanford Elementary each year. This active leadership brought about a higher level of involvement. This has led to more roles that empower parents as advocates. Parents now have more knowledge of the programs and rigorous curriculums that are being taught at their children's schools.

Activities That Increase Parent Engagement

Many school districts have developed parent training programs to help parents improve their parenting skills so that children can come to school better prepared. Under the No Child Left Behind (NCLB) Act, Section 1118 mandates that schools provide parent training instruction as home activities to support student learning. Parent-U-Turn found that when parents are trained on the curriculum that is taught in their children's school, the student's performance rate improves. This increases confidence and in turn, motivates children to perform better.

How Comprehensive Do Parent Engagement Efforts Need to Be?

Parents can become engaged through training and social activities. Once parents are engaged with knowledge, respected and treated as equal partners, they are more likely to be involved in their child's education. Schools can also eliminate the barriers that prevent parents from being involved, such as the lack of childcare and transportation to get to school. Parent-U-Turn calls for a different model of schooling, one in which parents are involved as equal partners.

While some schools have adopted comprehensive efforts to increase parental participation, relatively few steps have actually been taken in this area. The NCLB Act has forced districts to engage parents as equal partners. The "three-way compact" is one example of a tool that promotes equal partnership roles. The compact must be signed by the principal, teacher, and parent, and provides roles for each stakeholder for student academic progress. The Parent School Compact document was used to hold parents and students accountable for certain actions or lack thereof. Parents and students signed the three-way compact when they attended back-to-school night with teachers. The only problem with the three-way compact is that the teachers never sign the compact; instead the principal signs on the line for teachers. Teachers refuse to sign the compact because they are afraid that the document could be used against them. It is not mandated that parents sign the compact. The main purpose of the three-way compact is to show partnership between school and family as partners in child education.

Parent Engagement and Grade Level

There appears to be a positive relationship between the age of the child and the forms of parent engagement. Greater efforts to involve parents are seen at the elementary school levels. Schools focus on encouraging parents to assist children in the classroom and reading to them at home. Parents of young children are the most frequent visitors to schools, and we have found a higher level of parent engagement at the elementary grade level. At the middle and high school levels, parent involvement practices have declined because of the lack of outreach. Parent engagement at this level needs to be more supported and encouraged. Families often have both parents working. This fact gives schools greater responsibility for the achievement of their students. Some students are bused in from neighborhood schools, and parents are less able to spend time at the school because of this distance. The majority of high schools mandate that teachers are responsible for reaching out to students' parents.

At the secondary level, Parent Liaisons practice home visits. This position seems to have a positive effect in increasing parent involvement. Parents can play a major role in restricting television viewing, video games, and other distractions that take the focus away from homework assignments. Parents must advocate for their children to get beyond high school and into college. Parent-U-Turn has found that students who drop out reported that their parents rarely helped them with homework. Parent-U-Turn has collected data on student dropout rates by surveying and interviewing both parents and students. The surveys and interviews were conducted from 2003 through 2004 at the secondary level. There were several schools that participated in this study, including South Gate High, Lynwood High, and South Gate Middle School in the Los Angeles Unified School District. The results of the study showed that the children of parents who had negative contact with their school were more likely to drop out. These parents were more likely to work long hours at their jobs. The majority of parents interviewed said they spent little time engaging their high school students to make educational decisions.

While the majority of secondary teachers felt that parent involvement is important at the high school level, only 3 out of 10 teachers reached out to parents in a friendly way. PUT conducted a survey with teachers at South Gate High in 2005 on the importance of parent involvement. Also, our interviews and work with teachers in preservice teacher programs reflected the same results. Increasing two-way communication between home and school was proven to create an environment for building relationships. Most teachers in the high schools reported that they lacked the time to pursue outreach to parents. A Parent-U-Turn report that was generated from parents of high school students stated that the parents felt that they have little or no idea about what is happening in their children's schools. Parents felt that they know more about their children's education during elementary school than in high school. Parent-U-Turn also found that teens are less likely to want their parents to volunteer at their school. PUT also found that students in elementary school love to have their parents on campus.

Urban Parents Recasting the Idea of Parent Engagement

My goal in this section of the chapter is to improve on Joyce Epstein's (1995, 2002) model of parent involvement and to create a new model of parent engagement that includes *all* parents in the 21st century. It has been my experience as a parent of color living in a multicultural and urban working class area of the United States that Epstein's model, which is often cited by school officials as the definitive word in parent involvement, is not appropriate for our needs. It also fails to take into consideration our potential and draws on the assumption that the school must always be the one to bring us in, to entertain us, and to provide for us. In other words, this model disempowers parents of color from the potential we have to create change in our schools.

The model of parent engagement that I will lay out comes from my work with Parent-U-Turn (PUT) and the LAUSD Parent Collaborative. I worked with fellow members of these groups to create seven different elements that we feel are needed and necessary to move urban working class parents and communities of color from audience members to active participants. The model presented here is the first document created by these parents regarding what is needed to become advocates for our children. These seven elements will help empower parents of color to make informed decisions about the education, safety, and health of their children in urban and underperforming schools.

This book proves the efficacy of our program in that it is the first time an urban parent of color has written a document to engage and aid parents in navigating the educational system in an effort to improve student achievement.

It's the Law

If a school receives Title 1 federal funds to boost achievement in low-income areas, the No Child Left Behind Act requires the school and the district to involve parents in developing both parent engagement policies and school improvement. Research provides overwhelming evidence that parent involvement promotes children's academic achievement.

Under No Child Left Behind, parents have the right to be equal partners. We needed bottom-up accountability to make the schools treat parents in a respectful way. Now we had a best practice that aligns with NCLB Section 1118 that brings parents engagement into the 21st century.

When recasting Joyce Epstein's six principles, we used her model as a guide. However, we included what we felt she left out and created what we, as parents of color, believe all parents need in order to successfully navigate our children beyond high school and into college. These are the seven elements/steps, and they are to be directed at parents from urban and rural working class communities. I am not an expert in rural community schooling, but these steps are resources for best practices for all communities.

Examples of the Seven Steps of Engagement

Seven examples that include voices from parents and community organizers are as follows:

- Step 1: *Parent's Access to School Information and Data Collection.* Parents need to have access to timely and accurate information regarding their children's education in order to best support their children's academic success.
- Step 2: *Parents in Decision-Making Roles.* Parents provide leadership in schools by being at the table with teachers and administrators.
- Step 3: *Parents as Student Advocates.* Parents need to know how to navigate and negotiate the school system. We need to support the

creation of an environment where parents have access to information and support systems to be effective advocates by monitoring and directing the education of our children.

▪ Step 4: *Parent Leaders at Home and in the School-Community*. Parents need opportunities to build leadership and advocacy skills to enhance student–parent–community partnerships. Schools will serve the family and community needs for health and social services, which include providing resources and information for accessing those services.

▪ Step 5: *Effective Two–Way Communication*. Communication must be translated into languages that parents speak in their home. Plus, communication between home and school should be frequent, go both ways, and be meaningful.

▪ Step 6: *District-Level Support*. The district needs to provide structures to build parent capacity that are well-defined, including meaningful participation and dialogue that empowers parents for action and movement toward critical components of educational reform.

▪ Step 7: *Friendly School Atmosphere*. Schools should build an atmosphere that welcomes all parents and builds positive relationships.

Seven-Steps Framework in Practice: Stories of Implementation From Parents

This section describes the framework of the seven types of parent and community organization. It also focuses on parents involvement and action approaches in the implementation of practice. The reports include the experiences of parent leaders and community organizers who work in urban schools with Academic Performance Index (API) scores ranging from 1 to 3. These ideas and experiences document the practitioner's involvement in the continuing improvement of roles for authentic 21st-century parent engagement.

2

Step 1:
Parents' Access to School Information and Data Collection

Gathering Data on Year-Round Schools versus Traditional School Calendar

Los Angeles Unified School District
South Gate, California

Parents need to have access to timely and accurate information in order to best support their children's academic success. This includes

- Parents using, analyzing, and collecting data about their schools;
- Parents understanding data and using data that drives reform efforts;
- Parents becoming empowered to investigate and document conditions in their schools by becoming researchers in their own communities;
- Parent access to information about the resources and rights to support their children.

The 21st Century Parent, pages 11–13
Copyright © 2012 by Information Age Publishing

11

Figure 2.1   Parents becoming advocates for their children against a year-round school calendar.

In 2005, the LAUSD proposed the addition of another track of students to the already overcrowded schools in southeast Los Angeles. With this change, students would lose more instructional hours, and teachers would not have permanent classrooms. Parents saw how additional tracks would decrease the quality of their students' schools, and they decided to take a stand against year-round schooling. Parents worked with author Jeannie Oakes, and they began to research and collect data to support their stance against year-round schooling.

The data that parents and community members collected about Concept 6 year-round schooling was presented to school officials in April of 2005 at a LAUSD board meeting. The data collected led parents of Stanford Elementary to organize a movement to return schools in South Gate back to a traditional calendar after 25 years of being on the Concept 6 calendar. The data were presented to board members at a board meeting, and parents gave the district other options. About 350 to 400 Stanford Elementary parents attended this meeting. This overwhelming attendance in opposition to the added track caused the district to back off.

Parents and community members used the data collected to push for a traditional calendar. The data showed that children were missing 17 days of instruction a year on the Concept 6 schedule. Concept 6 students were going to school for 163 days compared to the traditional calendar of 180 days. The conclusion was that if our children attended Concept 6 schools from grades 1 to 12, they would lose 204 days of instruction. Parents realized that their children would have lost one full year of instruction time. The data was collected, and because parents had the knowledge to interpret and analyze this information, they were able to make a great impact on the student school schedule and ultimately student achievement.

Epstein's (1990) six-part typology for parent involvement has become well known among educators as basic for outreach. In Epstein's *Six Key Steps*, she does not mention anything regarding data collection. We currently live in a data-driven society, and failure to acknowledge this has left parents of color at a huge disadvantage. Step 1 in our model also aligned with NCLB Section 1118, and the California School Accountability Report Card (SARC). This standard is also driven by the principle that an informed parent is a powerful parent for social change.

STEPS TAKEN TO WIN THE CONCEPT 6 ISSUE

1. Parents conducted research to support their perspective
2. Parents collaborated with a university professor
3. Parents presented data to the school board
4. Parents rallied 350–400 other parents to attend the board meetings

3

Step 2: Parents in Decision-Making Roles

Parents Take On New Roles

Lynwood Unified School District
Lynwood, California

By providing leadership in schools by participating with teachers and administrators in multiple ways, parents help themselves and their students. When parents actively set policies and are involved in key decisions with school leaders, they ensure that schools have adequate resources to carry out their missions and obligations. Parents can also provide training and evaluation of school structures. Finally, decision making must incorporate input from families and the community. The activities that create effective parent participation include

- Participating in local advisory committees with genuine parent participation;
- Working on effective advocacy and education as a direct result of understanding how systems are structured (e.g., how decisions

The 21st Century Parent, pages 15–18
Copyright © 2012 by Information Age Publishing
All rights of reproduction in any form reserved.

and power are distributed among schools, staff, parents, and students);

▪ Providing other parents with knowledge, skills, and opportunities to actively engage them in all levels of the decision-making process;

▪ Representing parents on the school decision-making teams.

Figure 3.1   Parents at Hosler Middle gaining knowledge on research issues surrounding schooling.

From 1997 to 2000, Lynwood parents moved from playing the traditional parent involvement roles. This change began when parents and community members went through UCLA's Parent Project, a parent professional development program that educated parents on student's rights. Through the UCLA Parent Project, over 600 parents were educated in "what good teaching looks like." Parents were empowered with knowledge about the curriculum and policies that govern schools. After participating in this professional development program, parents began mentoring other parents.

When parents and community members graduated from the program, they became very active in school councils. Meetings were then conducted using Robert's Rules of Order. Also, as a result of the training, many parents began to act as mentors in different subjects, such as reading and writing School Accountability Report Card (SARC) reports, looking for a rigorous academic curriculum, and reading data and policies that govern schools. Parents were able to participate as equal partners on school councils because of their skills in reading data and their knowledge about curriculum and instruction. These parents' newly found leadership skills brought a new meaning to parents as equal partners in the decision-making process.

Figure 3.2 Parents learning how to read data.

Joyce Epstein addresses decision making in her six types of parent involvement. However her view of decision making is too general; it lacks content or suggestions on what it should look like in practice. In other words, it is left open to interpretation, thus exclusively in the hands of academics rather than practitioners. This lack of clarity leaves too much up to school authorities to decide what decision making should look like.

Summary

Recommendation for Parent Involvement

- Elect strong parent representatives
- Attend School Site Council and English Language Advisory Council meetings. Make sure to attend some district board meetings.
- Acquire data by conducting surveys and from instructional materials and school data.
- Get to know the decision makers at your school: the principal and members of your School Site Council (SSC), School Advisory

Council (Title1) and English Language Advisory Committee (ELAC).

- If you're dissatisfied with the school's actions, ask parents on the School Site Council not to approve any funding requests and let other parents know why.
- File a Uniform Complaint Procedures form.
- Work with parents to develop parent involvement policies and publicize these to parents in a language and format they understand.

Things were bad, but we did not know how bad. For example, parents thought teachers were credentialed but later we learned that 65% of the teachers at our schools were not credentialed.

—Valerie Munoz, Parent-U-Turn

4

Step 3: Parents as Student Advocates

Parent as Advocates and Experts

Los Angeles Unified School District
Los Angeles, California

Parents need to know how to navigate and negotiate the school system. We need to support the creation of an environment where parents have access to information and support systems and to be effective advocates who monitor and direct the education of our children. Among other things, parents need to

- Know what children need, how to access resources, and how to implement a plan of action;
- Understand how to make and use a power map detailing the functions and structures of the system;
- Understand and be able to communicate in an educational setting, using terms used by educational professionals.

The 21st Century Parent, pages 19–22
Copyright © 2012 by Information Age Publishing

Parents across southeast Los Angeles County offer striking examples of collaboration with schools and elected officials. Parents serve as advocates, encouraging elected officials and others to think about the interests of all children. Their advocacy training holds all officials accountable in guaranteeing that all students have equal access to a quality education.

Parent-U-Turn and Students meeting with Speaker of House Assemblyman Fabian Nunez.

Community members and parents have put their experience to use by teaching other parents and students about school procedures and student rights. Parents help other parents and students by filling out different uniform complaint forms, Williams Settlement Complaint forms, and attending Individual Evaluation Process (IEP) meetings with parents and students as advocates in advisory roles. Also, parents in South Gate and Lynwood have held workshops on parent and student rights at local schools to enable other parents to keep the elected officials accountable.

Another example of parents serving as advocates occurred when Los Angeles City Attorney Rocky Delgadillo was concerned about the condition of restrooms in public schools. As a result of collaboration and training from Dr. John Rogers of UCLA's Institute for Democracy, Education, and Access (IDEA), parents in South Gate have a strong background in researching the cleanliness and condition of schools, including the restrooms, inside the Los Angeles Unified School District. Parents agreed with the elected officials that the overall condition of the school was often reflected in the condition of the restrooms. As a result of their training and advocacy, parents and the elected officials jointly developed a checklist for school facilities. On another occasion, parents in District 6 of the LAUSD

Parent-U-Turn's Mary Johnson and Mayor of Los Angeles, Antonio Villaraigosa

had been asked to speak as experts on the lack of textbooks and quality of teachers at a textbook hearing held at the LAUSD.

In my effort to support working class parents and increase their understanding of the public school system, I published *The Parent Survival Guide* in 2005. Its goal was to assist parents in navigating the school system in grades K–16. *The Parent Survival Guide*, sponsored by Congresswoman Linda Sanchez and written by urban parents who themselves have struggled in navigating the school system, is a map that parents of color can use to understand the ins and outs of the public school structure. For example, it breaks down the different offices at the school and their individual responsibilities, because most parents complain about how schools frequently send them from one office to another.

This guide also covers topics such as college preparation, scholarships and grants available for undocumented immigrants and African-American students, the ABCs of student success, special education, and information about how to work within the school structure. The guide also assists immigrant families and parents of color in finding support for their college-bound children with scholarship information, including names of organizations, requirements, contact information, and other needed information.

In 2007, it was my honor to receive an award on behalf of my L.A. Parent Advocate group from Loyola Marymount University. Loyola Marymount University recognizes me and my membership for our success and commitment to our advocacy for children, particularly those in special education.

Our Step 3 of parent engagement is not addressed often in other parent involvement models such as Epstein, Comer, and such. For all too long scholars have provided limited perception of who we are as parent of color from working class communities (Comer, 1955; Epstein, 2002) We argue that parents from working class communities need to know how to engage professional educators if they are going to be public participants in their children's education. Only when parents understand the school structure and policies that govern schools, and particularly the language of education, can they hold the system accountable.

Summary

Strategies for Parent Advocacy

- Understand the No Child Left Behind Act and how it works in your state.
- Visit schools in pairs for support and to help document conversations.
- Join local parent groups like Parent-U-Turn; also, contact national Civil Rights groups (advocacy services and information regarding parents/students rights, special education issues and racial discrimination), or form your own group.
- Educate yourself about your child's school. Check out the school report cards that compare schools. Make a list of items you need more information on.
- Know the rights of children as students and of parents concerning taking off work time to attend school activities.
- Know how to write complaints and hold people accountable.
- Build partnerships.
- Gain knowledge on research issues surrounding schooling.

5

Step 4: Parent Leaders at Home and in the School-Community

Parents as Parent Educators

Parents need opportunities to build leadership and advocacy skills to enhance student-parent-community partnerships. Schools can serve the family and community needs for health and social services and provide resources and information for accessing those services when parents are involved. With support, parents will achieve the following:

- Learning intergenerational and cross-cultural communication strategies with a special emphasis fon immigrant families.
- Discovering "21st-century parenting skills," such as how to develop boundaries, parent-child communication, identifying risk factors (e.g., drugs and gang involvement).
- Understanding requirements and financial-aid processes.
- Developing meeting facilitation, public speaking, conflict resolution, and cross-cultural training.

The 21st Century Parent, pages 23–26
Copyright © 2012 by Information Age Publishing
All rights of reproduction in any form reserved.

- Practicing communication for navigating their children through K–12 to college.
- Receiving ongoing support and technical assistance to equip them for effective participation.

Parents have become educators of parents and teachers. Above, Mary Johnson, along with a Title 1 expert in LAUSD, discusses with preservice teachers Title 1 funding and its uses in schools.

In 1999, parents developed their own 13-week parent curriculum and served as facilitators and directors of parent workshops. These programs are about engaging parents with the curriculum that their children are being taught at school. Parents are put in classroom settings similar to the setting that their children are in while at school. Then they are instructed about state standards and policies that govern how schools are run. The result is that parents become empowered with knowledge about their children's schools. These parent leaders hold schools accountable to ensure that all children have equal access to a quality education and programs, regardless of family income.

After completion of the 13-week program, students and family members are invited to the graduation, and in most instances, this is the parent's first graduation. The goal of the parent curriculum course is that the new feeling of accomplishment will shift down to their children. The purpose is to break the cycle of negativity that surrounds urban schooling and the fears that make schools a low priority.

Parents have not only become facilitators of parents and community members, but they have also played an important role in educating and training teachers about parent involvement.

Parents who graduate from the PUT program have the opportunity to complete follow-up assistance in which they are supported while becoming a facilitator at their school or in their community. Parents work with others to develop planning and utilize resources that allow them to successfully duplicate the workshop in their communities so that parents can go on educating other parents on how to successfully navigate from K–12 school structures into universities.

Epstein does discuss parent roles, but it is limited in content and context. There is no room in Epstein's model to broaden the content to go beyond homework *and* address urban parents' needs. Parents in urban schools need equal intervention resources in the areas of gang influences, drug problems, and criminal activities, all of which go beyond basic parenting skills.

Key to Success: Unity

Getting school districts to listen to parents wasn't easy. For example, 10 to 25 members of Parent-U-Turn participated in meetings with the district superintendent, a local newspaper reporter, and our state Assembly member regarding violation of NCLB Section 1118. We also called and faxed the California Department of Education. In the end, the district agreed to a legally binding contract-containing 34 parental engagement requirements. The real change occurs when parents come together.

Summary

Open Door Strategies for Parents

- Knowledge about course requirements and the curriculum used in the classroom;
- Understanding how to read data from Standardized Testing and Reporting (STAR) testing and other school assessments;
- Collect data through surveys, focus groups, and assessments;
- Mediate interactions between parents and community.

6

Step 5: Effective Two-Way Communication

Best Practices for School Districts

Communication in multicultural and multilingual communities must be translated into languages that parents speak in their home. Communication between home and school must not only be a regular, two-way occurrence, it also has to be relevant and meaningful. These multicultural and multilingual ways of communicating with parents must include, but not be limited to, computers, newsletters, personal contact, letters/flyers, and the school marquee. Parent Liaison roles in multicultural schools must also help bridge communication between the school and home and help create effective home/school relationships. This includes the cultural awareness to be able to work with parents of diverse cultural, linguistic, and economic backgrounds and experiences. In many urban and multicultural communities, the Parent Liaison role is the key to fostering relationships with parents and open communication between schools and communities. There is, however, no relationship more important than that between parents and teachers, and that is the idea behind *The Urban Parent Teacher Education Collaborative.*

The 21st Century Parent, pages 27–30
Copyright © 2012 by Information Age Publishing
All rights of reproduction in any form reserved.

Teachers must be willing to communicate with parents through multiple media.

The Urban Parent Teacher Education Collaborative is a pioneering model for universities. By creating a space for a university professor and a grass-roots parent organizer to team-teach a class for preservice teachers, Pepperdine University has recognized parents as experts in the area of how and what is needed to educate children in urban schools. This new model allows future teachers to have contact with urban parents before they come into our school communities. In workshops, preservice teachers are given strategies for interacting with parents in order to learn how to build a working relationship with them. For example, PUT members and teachers practice role reversals that allow both teachers and parents to acquire a better understanding and respect for the importance of each other's roles.

This distinct model of teacher education seeks to build a clinical laboratory for teacher preparation driven by parent involvement with the following goals:

- To increase and sustain teachers' knowledge, skills, and positive attitudes toward families through their participation in a community dialogue forum with urban parents;
- To move beyond classroom-based teaching methods by offering teachers direct field experience working with families;

- To enable preservice teachers to develop effective practices to prepare their work with families and communities;
- To establish a context for preservice teachers to learn about urban communities;
- To increase working relationships between novice resident teachers with families and students that breaks down perceptions of stereotypes and improves student achievement;
- To assist Parent Liaisons in working with all races of people.

Summary

All schools should consider the following strategies:

- Communicate in languages that parents speak in their home.
- Encourage regular, two-way, meaningful conversation between the school and home.
- Advocate communication utilizing computers, newsletters, personal contact, letters, flyers, and a marquee.

BUILDING MULTIRACIAL RELATIONSHIPS: EDUCATIONAL JUSTICE FOR ONE COMMON HUMANITY

I created the following pledge for membership in the Parent Collaborative. There was a strong need to unite African American and Latino parents in the Los Angeles Unified School District. Parents were divided by racial lines, and the division and conflicts stopped any progress in moving the students' agenda at the meetings.

PLEDGE

We parents and leaders believe that the strength of California lies in its diversity. We are committed to building strong relationships among all parents—relationships that demonstrate acceptance, respect, and trust. Strong relationships across racial lines are important for several reasons. First, all parents in California want a quality education for their children. We can best accomplish this goal by working together as one. Second, when parents are not divided, they can draw on one another's strengths. Parents acting in unison develop skills and power to improve their communities. Third, parents are their children's first teachers. When parents model positive multiracial relationships, they provide their children with a vision of a multiracial democracy.

CREANDO RELACIONES ENTRE TODAS LAS RAZAS JUSTICIA EDUCATIVA PARA UNA HUMANIDAD EN COMÚN

JURAMENTO

Nosotros, los padres y líderes, sabemos que la fortaleza de California, está en su diversidad. Estamos comprometidos a crear relaciones fuertes entre todos los padres—relaciones que demuestren aceptación, respeto y confianza. Las relaciones fuertes entre todas las razas son importantes por varias razones. Primero, los padres de California desean una educación de calidad para sus hijos. Podemos alcanzar esta meta de la mejor manera al trabajar en unidad. Segundo, cuando los padres no están divididos, se pueden beneficiar de las fortalezas de unos y otros. Los padres que actúan en unidad desarrollan destrezas y adquieren poder para mejorar sus comunidades. Tercero, los padres son los primeros maestros de sus hijos. Cuando los padres son modelo de relaciones positivas entre diferentes razas, dan a sus hijos un vistazo de la democracia multirracial.

Name/Nombre: _____

School/Escuela: _____

7

Step 6: District-Level Support

The school district must support parents' structures. It is often repeated in parent circles that school and district staff are following district directives and have vested interests in preserving the status quo rather than in training parent leaders to become advocates for their children. The Local Education Agency is responsible for setting up the model and structure that build the foundation for parents to participate at the local school site. This kind of professional development for parents is created and developed with the assistance of Title 1 parents and the English Learner Parent committee. This committee is comprised of parents of English Language Learners. ELAC advise the principal and school staff on programs and services for English Language Learners. There is money set aside for parent involvement at the district level. The parent involvement allocation set aside is a minimum of 1% and a maximum of 5%. To get the maximum allocation of 5%, you must justify the need for training for the parents.

The Local Educational Agency must provide parents training to build parent capacity that is well-defined, and where meaningful participation such as dialogue, empowerment, and action are critical components of educational reform. This mid-level structure will be fully funded by Title 1 and led by parent councils that will ensure that the training is provided to all

The 21st Century Parent, pages 31–34
Copyright © 2012 by Information Age Publishing
All rights of reproduction in any form reserved.

parents in a friendly environment and is also culturally friendly. Leadership training topics may include

- Providing parents with training and capacity-building opportunities to effectively engage in school reform at the local and district level;
- Providing parents with information and resources to meet the needs of the whole child;
- Enabling parents to support students and school programs;
- Providing training to support their children through a discussion with teachers regarding how to engage their children and families;
- Training on how to volunteer in their school, how to navigate the school system, and how to advocate for the benefit of children;
- Training on parental responsibilities, such as information on how to help your child with homework, how to participate in a parent-teacher conference, and knowing the A–G requirements (classes required for university entrance);
- Training about parental and student rights so that they can be advocates for their children;
- Training on how to collect, analyze, and use data about their schools for effective advocacy;
- Training on school budgets, advisory committees, school councils, and leadership teams to be equal partners in decision making on campus.

Los Angeles Unified Schools have modified parent involvement for the 21st century. Parents have moved from traditional roles of being parent

Organizing bake sales and small fundraisers no longer suffice for parent involvement.

Parents *must* be decision makers, leaders, researchers, advocates, trainers, and educators.

fundraisers, hall monitors, and bathroom monitors to facilitators of leadership workshops. Now, in the 21st century, the LAUSD has included parents as partners in the accountability process to make sure that parents are equal partners in every local school and at the district level. The Parent Involvement Strategies Plan includes the Urban Recasting Model for leadership. This is the first set of frameworks written by parents of the LAUSD whose students attend API 1–3 schools. Additionally, this is the first framework written by a parent in the nation.

The parent committee of the LAUSD also conducted a parent survey across the LAUSD. Parents and Los Angeles Unified School board members are committed and dedicated to the effort of parent-led surveys of parents across the LAUSD. The parents generated the survey questions and have the last say on what is on the survey and when the survey is given.

Another example of how parent roles have changed is in the area of parent involvement with the development and presentation in decision making at the schools alongside staff, the teacher's union, and the principal's union on the role of School Site Councils. This plan has parents moving from fundraisers and hall monitors to facilitators and cheerleaders to empower and inspire other parents to promote early involvement in their children's education. In the past, a Parent Child Abuse Prevention subcommittee had been trained in a program called Darkness to Light, a Child Abuse Prevention Program, and is now going out as the facilitators and presenters of the program across the LAUSD.

We acknowledge that Epstein's six types of parent involvement engage the issue of parent participation at the district level, including the establishment of "independent advocacy groups," which will serve to lobby for school reform and improvements (National Network of Partnership Schools, 2006). Our Step 6 aligns loosely with Epstein's Type 5 of parental involvement.

Summary

School districts should consider the following strategies:

- Hold parent meetings at times convenient for parents, providing transportation, childcare, or home visits, if necessary;
- Hold an annual meeting for parents, explaining the school's participation in Title 1, and let parents know they have a right to be involved;
- Work with parents to develop a parent involvement policy and publicize it to parents in a language and format they understand;
- Conduct workshops on course requirements and the curriculum used in the classroom;
- Survey parent needs.

8

Step 7: Friendly Schools Atmosphere

The school atmosphere must be welcoming to parents. Research has proven that when parents feel welcomed on campuses, they will be more involved. Posting welcome signs throughout the school in languages other than English help immigrant parents feel welcome. When the staff provides mandatory customer service training and parents fill out surveys, they become more engaged in the school.

Southeast Los Angeles middle schools and many others schools in the LAUSD posted signs throughout their campuses in many languages. The LAUSD created a welcome committee to investigate welcoming atmospheres at schools. The committee concluded that schools needed to provide mandatory customer service training every year for the entire school staff. Another recommendation was that parents and other stakeholders fill out a survey on services rendered.

Some districts in California use the same concept in sales and send "mystery shoppers" to schools. The mystery individual is a person who evaluates the services given. He/she writes up a report and submits it back to their department. Then a letter is written and sent to the principals. An

The 21st Century Parent, pages 35–36
Copyright © 2012 by Information Age Publishing
All rights of reproduction in any form reserved.

example of how the majority of Los Angeles schools have begun to create a friendly school atmosphere is the volunteer greeters or employees that most people encounter when first entering a school.

The greeter's roles are to help to create a friendly atmosphere for visitors by guiding them to the appropriate office(s) for services. At the front kiosk, there needs to be a customer service box so all stakeholders may leave their comments regarding the customer service at the school. Ideally, the box must be open, and the comments must be read at the principal's meetings twice a month. Practitioners have documented that the number-one reason principals take the appropriate action and notify the stakeholders to find solutions to complaints are the comments from parents. It is important that parents have an opportunity to give feedback if they do not attend meetings or visit the schools as a result of not feeling welcome.

In friendly schools, parents need to be involved with the school in decision-making committees. The Parent-U-Turn organization uses the NCLB Section 1118 requirement to demand a-change toward a friendly school culture. It is also a process with the schools, districts, administrators and support staff that requires both trust and collaboration.

A friendly school culture was also left out of Epstein's six keys that were adopted by the State of California. The number-one complaint from parents in urban schools is that the school staff is rude and unfriendly. This is the major reason parents give for not participating or volunteering at the local school.

Summary

Administrators should consider the following strategies:

- Encourage parents to volunteer in the school, and observe and participate in their children's classes;
- Work with parents to develop a school-parent "compact" spelling out parent and school responsibilities;
- Send parent comments to the school district if parents aren't satisfied with the school's educational plan;
- Provide annual customer service training to all support staff personnel and teachers.
- Interview parents and the school community about school issues.

9

What Should Be Done Next?

It is now time to come up with standards for parent involvement. We have standards for everything in California, except for parent engagement. Today, the State of California and the federal government require standards for holding schools accountable for our children. I believe that it is time to develop a document or set of procedures that can fully implement the intention of the NCLB Section 1118 parent involvement.

The parent standards will help to make authentic roles for parents. Parent involvement needs to move to another level. If parents are going to be equal to teachers in the campaign for school reform, we need to include their voices in the evaluation process.

Parent standards should seek to encourage, enable, and maintain a positive and effective relationship between the parent community and school staff. The following suggestions are evidence of what real participation would look like if parents had authentic roles. The purpose of the policy would be to promote joint collaboration between the parent community and school services, thus maintaining a safe school environment. This includes

The 21st Century Parent, pages 37–38
Copyright © 2012 by Information Age Publishing

- Assisting in the greater safety and protection of students in schools;
- Enabling the larger parent community to have a voice in decision making in local schools;
- Encouraging ongoing, adaptive, and responsive relationships between the parent community and schools;
- Facilitating appropriate sharing and disclosure of school conditions;
- Ensuring that the intentions and requirements of both the NCLB and California State Accountability Report Card systems are met;
- Ensuring a consistent approach across local school districts in the way parents and community members engage in the accountability process.

Summary to Consider for All LEAs (Local Education Agency)

- Provide a space for organizations to share ideas and strategies.
- Provide advanced training to engage parents in advocacy.
- Conduct independent analysis of policies affecting parents.
- Provide a forum for stakeholder groups to express their concerns and issues.

10

Summary of Parent Groups' Success in the Seven-Steps Principle

Access to Information and Data Collection

PUT is an example of how urban parents can use data collection to make changes for their children as a result of taking research seriously. Parent-U-Turn has engaged in a variety of participatory research projects in recent years exploring the conditions of schools and the history of the struggle for educational equity. Our members have developed surveys around our school conditions and presented them to local officials. We have gathered data from parents of students who attend schools in our district and used these survey results to change the conditions of the schools that our children attend. Parent-U-Turn members in the past have also attended monthly UCLA/IDEA meetings to study school conditions and learn research skills. Our organization believes that the data we collect will document and verify how these conditions affect our students, both academically and socially. PUT's ability to research issues of access to quality education is the only way to change our community and promote a safe and effective educational environment for all students. The skills that PUT members have ac-

The 21st Century Parent, pages 39–44
Copyright © 2012 by Information Age Publishing

quired by using surveys to organize parents around school conditions have helped parents monitor and evaluate schools under the LAUSD and LUSD.

For example, PUT was able to advocate for a traditional school calendar rather than the Concept 6 year-round schooling schedule. Through our research, we were able to show that Concept 6 didn't do anything to improve student achievement. Concept 6's only benefit is to relieve overcrowding. Students that were on the Concept 6 calendar missed a total of 17 days a year. In our communities, schools have been on the Concept 6 calendar for 25 years. This means that when a student from grades 1–12 graduates from one of these schools he/she will have lost approximately 10,140 hours or 204 days of instructional time. This is one of the many reasons why our urban students aren't bridging the achievement gap between children of color as well as non–children of color. In most instances, when our children begin kindergarten, they are already 850 vocabulary words behind. Up until the 2005–2006 school year, schools in Black and Latino neighborhoods were on a half-day schedule, while kindergarten classes in non-colored neighborhoods have always been on full days.

Still, most schools in overcrowded neighborhoods are on half days due to a lack of space. Other barriers that our surveys have shown include a lack of textbooks, facilities, and quality teachers. After gathering data, we came to the conclusion that all schools had similar or the same problems. Some of the primary problems were that they did not have enough restrooms, materials, credentialed teachers, and school counselors. Most parents believed that their children weren't getting a quality education. Surveys done at shopping malls reflected our belief that not all students have access to a quality education. Some of this research has been published in IDEA's online journal at www.TeachingToChangeLA.org.

Parents in Decision-Making Roles

Our advocacy in the areas of education and student rights has helped PUT to hold both the Los Angeles Unified School District and the Lynwood Unified School District accountable. On September 15, 2004, Parent-U-Turn was able to write the Lynwood District up for 34 violations with uniform complaints regarding the restriction of parents from participating as equal decision makers in their children's schooling. Every complaint that we wrote up was based on NCLB Section 1118 or the California ED CODE that governs schools. We, as parents, brought our grievances to the California State Department of Education, which mandated that the Lynwood School District resolve these complaints. This led to the district's first ever Resolution Agreement with a parent organization. We now use this Resolution Agreement as outside evaluators. Parent-U-Turn's agreement is a part of the Local Educational Agency's single plan that governs all of the district's schools.

Community Asset Development Re-Defining Education (CADRE), another grassroots organization located in south central Los Angeles, has an ongoing practice of organizing and canvassing door-to-door, typically in neighborhoods and homes, as a way of engaging parents as they come to action campaigns. Parents also make decisions about organizing and developing their leadership hands-on. CADRE focuses on systemic policy changes at the district level rather than school-by-school for districtwide policy. Grassroots parents who don't work for the school determine the policies they campaign for.

Parents as Student Advocates

Parent-U-Turn is a strong multiracial organization. It offers a striking example of collaboration between Black and Latino parents in Los Angeles. The group encourages members to think about the interests of all students. Our organization's members attend Individual Evaluation Process (IEP) meetings and other meetings that put parents in advisory roles. We are accessible to parents in South Gate and Los Angeles County. Parent-U-Turn holds trainings on parent and student rights at local schools. Our advocacy holds all officials accountable for guaranteeing that all students have equal access to a quality education.

Parent-U-Turn members and other parents have put their training to use by teaching other parents about school procedures and student rights. Parents help other parents by filling out uniform complaints and attending IEP meetings with parents as advocates. We are no longer *asking* for accountability; we are now *demanding* it. We are teaching parents that it's okay to take on school districts and demand changes. For instance, our advocacy in this area has helped PUT to hold both the Los Angeles Unified School District and the Lynwood Unified School District to bottom-up accountability.

On September 15, 2004, Parent-U-Turn was able to write the Lynwood District up for 34 violations with uniform complaints regarding the restriction of parents from participating as equal decision makers in their children's schooling. Every complaint that we wrote up was based on NCLB Section 1118 or the California ED CODE that governs schools. We, as parents, brought our grievances to the State Department of Education, which mandated that the Lynwood School District resolve these complaints. This led to the district's first ever Resolution Agreement with a parent organization. We now use this Resolution Agreement as outside evaluators. Parent-U-Turn's agreement is a part of the Local Educational Agency's single plan that governs all of the district's schools. This allows us to ensure that Lynwood Unified schools stay in compliance in the area of resolution. Parent-U-Turn serves the needs and defends the rights of individuals with disabilities and their families. Parent-U-Turn spends significant time and resources meeting and advocating for families for the last ten years.

Effective Two-Way Communication at the South Gate High School Parent Center

In South Gate, Parent Liaisons make flyers for parents in English and Spanish to meet the needs of the community. After flyers are sent out, liaisons make personal contact with parents for meetings and events. Plus, the liaison uses Connect ED to dial parents on upcoming school events. The Parent Center is the room that serves parent needs and from where Parent Liaisons send out monthly calendars for events and workshops. Parents can call the Parent Center regarding concerns and school events. When the center is closed, there is a message machine, and liaisons follow up on messages the next working day. The Parent Center is staffed by volunteers and paid staff employees.

Guidelines for Parent Centers on School Sites in the 21st Century

Parent Centers support structures for parent engagement.

──────────

Three Levels of Parent Structures for 21st Century Parent Centers

The following explains the necessary strategies for creating a successful hub, building trust and relationship between parents and school staff.

1. Building local parent capacity: In order to build parent engagement, it is important to help parents navigate the school system. For example, it is important to provide the parents the proper tools for success in parent counseling for behavioral problems. During these workshops, parents will be taught how to actively engage and seek individual and collective strength to address issues and improve conditions on school campuses. These opportunities will provide parents with the leadership and governance skills they need to better their community and to
    – Help navigate the school system,

    – Provide parent counseling,
    – Support individual and collective parent efforts to address issues and improve conditions on campuses,
    – Provide parents leadership and governance skills training.
2. Parent space will
    – Provide space for parent organizations to share ideas/strategies,
    – Provide advanced training to engage parents in advocacy,
    – Conduct independent analysis of policies affecting children,
    – Provide forums for groups to express their concerns/issues.
3. Parent hubs will
    – Act as an information clearinghouse for school programs,
    – Be a place to refer parents to social services agencies,
    – Be available as a research center for parents,
    – Be available to give information and resources to parents and community members on school data.

The Los Angeles County Office of Education recognized the South Gate High Parent Center for being effective in reaching out to parents and the community in 2008.

District-Level Supports

I was a Parent Liaison for the Lynwood Unified School District, where I was honored as an Outstanding Parent Trainer. I was employed with the district for 11 years. I began my journey working with parents of elementary school students. My job was to build a relationship between school and community by assembling a resource database for parents in the areas of academic and social services. As a parent, I knew if I wanted parents to volunteer, all barriers must be taken down. The first project was to change the school atmosphere to a friendly one where parents would feel welcome.

As Parent Liaison, my job was to make parents feel welcome and respected at my school. Another part of my job was to prepare parents to navigate the school structure. I encouraged parents to stand up for their children.

Friendly Schools Atmosphere

Parent-U-Turn used the parental involvement requirements of the federal No Child Left Behind Act to back up our demands for change. Even then, it was hard work. But in November 2002, the district signed an agreement creating new systems of parent involvement. For example, parents now sit on panels that interview applicants for teaching jobs. The district trains parents on understanding test scores and other school data, and schools must hold elections for parents who sit on decision-making panels. Now parents are sitting on the textbook committee. They are also sitting in on interviews. Parents are feeling welcomed at the school.

Conclusion

I believe that the attitudes and practices of minority parents toward the issues of involvement in their children's education vary. Some parents are concerned about their children's education and want to take on roles other than the traditional ones. Other parents who participated in focus groups expressed a high level of comfort by coming to school events and/or working with teachers when the atmosphere is user-friendly.

Schools must create a user-friendly atmosphere that parents can navigate as educational partners. School administrators and staff must perceive parents as a resource. To be a resource, the staff must respect the cultural wealth that families bring to their school. Schools that are serious about developing partnerships with parents can use this cultural wealth in the classroom curriculum.

Even as traditional approaches to partnership remain limited and school-centered, momentum has been building in some quarters for expanding the role of leadership and advocacy among parents, teachers, and principals in schools. Family and community engagement is increasingly seen as a powerful tool for making schools more equitable, culturally responsive, and collaborative, with leadership distributed across multiple stakeholders. This vision of school-community partnerships goes beyond traditional models geared mainly to school agendas or mandated collaboration. The goals of social justice education and democratic participation in schooling are the foundation for what we call "authentic school-community partnerships." These are respectful alliances among educators, families,

The 21st Century Parent, pages 45–46
Copyright © 2012 by Information Age Publishing

45

and community groups based on equity goals and marked by a willingness to engage in relationship building, dialogue, and power sharing. Though rare, such partnerships have sprung up in reform or experimental form in Los Angeles and elsewhere, with potential to effect change in urban schools.

Other Parent-U-Turn published articles can be found at www.Teaching ToChangeLA.org, Contact For Kids, *Children Advocate* magazine, and the National Coalition for Parent Involvement in Education (NCPIE). These articles include "Behind The Alameda Corridor" (www.Teaching ToChangeLA.org), "American Schools Have Failed Children of Color" (http://21stparent.com/), "Parents Becoming Researchers" (Teachers College Press), and "Parent In Charge" (Corwin).

Discussion Questions

1. What are the skills that are essential for urban and rural parents to develop in order to navigate the preschool to university system?
   - Knowledge of school structure;
   - Leadership and strategies solution;
   - Advocacy skills (Special Education, English Learner, etc.), parent and student rights in education codes, and federal law (NCLB or ED Codes);
   - Transition from each level: elementary/middle school and beyond to college;
   - Acroyln for 21st century.
   - Career readiness vs. college requirements (what the differences are between the two).
   - How to read and collect data to document barriers and conditions for their children's school;
   - What are state standards and curriculum per grade level of their children and how they are used in the classroom.

2. What are the skills that are essential for teachers to develop in order to be equipped and have a proactive relationship with parents as they work to develop the social and academic skills for their students?
   - High expectations for all students, regardless of race, disability, or the language that student speaks;
   - Understanding the barriers and challenges of the school community;

The 21st Century Parent, pages 47–48
Copyright © 2012 by Information Age Publishing

- Teachers must understand that every child or parent brings a unique resource to their classroom and school;
- Teachers must also remember that one model doesn't fix all parents and that outreach results will vary from one parent to another;
- Never give up trying, and be flexible on scheduling parent meetings;
- Write a quick note on student papers with positive remarks, so when they contact parents on others matters, parents are less inclined to be defensive.

3. How are Parent-U-Turn's seven steps of parent involvement different from Epstein's six types of parent involvement?
   - First, my model was written by parents of color, whose children attend schools in API ranges 1–3.
   - Parent-U-Turn has documented success stories of parents using the seven steps and how they implement these stages or steps in successful action for change.
   - The PUT model moves parents beyond the bake sales to advocacy.
   - The Epstein model is about parent involvement.
   - The Parent-U-Turn model is about parent engagement (a move for action).

Parent-U-Turn Publications and Media Coverage

Bottom-Up Accountability: Parents Can Use the No Child Left Behind Act to Get More of a Voice for Their Kids' Schools. Deborah Kong in Action Alliance for Children. November–December 2005. http://www.4children.org/news/1105ncle.htm

Activist Parent Writes Book on Dealing with Schools. Marcy Santana, Staff Writer for the *Los Angeles Wave* newspaper. September 7, 2005.

The Activist Parent. Adolfo Guzman Lopez profiles parents in the San Fernando Valley and in South Gate who are actively involved in their children's schools. KPCC talk Radio 89.3 (PUT). October 21, 2005. http://www.scpr.org/news/features/2005/10/fixing_our_schools.html

Every Student Deserves a Quality Teacher: Lynwood Parents Research Access to Quality Teachers. Mary Johnson, Parent Director of Parent-U-Turn, conducted interviews with assembly member Marco Firebaugh, congresswoman Juanita Millender-McDonald, and director of UCLA's Teacher Education Program, Eloise Lopez Metcalfe to determine what can be done to ensure quality teachers in Lynwood. Educational Bill of Rights. Vol. 2., Issue 3. http://tcla.gseis.ucla.edu/rights/features/3/johnson/

Building Parents as Researchers. Johnson, M., Munoz, V., & Street, E. (2003). ERIC ED478210. This paper describes a program in which parents learned about becoming educational researchers and developed research skills they could use for school improvement. Parent-U-Turn is a parent organization in Lynwood, California, and surrounding communities, which has worked with researchers from the University of California at Los Angeles to procure and gather information about quality schooling.

Acting on Our Rights. Johnson, M., & V. Munoz. An Educational Bill of Rights. Vol. 2., Issue 7. http://tcla.gseis.ucla.edu/rights/features/7/parents/johnson_munoz.html

Featured in:

Creating a Public Accountability for California Schools. Rogers, J. (2004). Teachers College Record: Teachers College, Columbia University (pp. 2171–2192).

First Things First: Why we must stop punishing student sand fix California's Schools. May 17, 2003. Californians for Justice. A report on school inequality and the impact of the California High School Exit Exam. http://www.caljustice.org/pdf/first_things_first.pdf

Recommended Reading

Rogers, J. (2006). Forces of accountability? The power of poor parents in No Child Left Behind. *Harvard Educational Review, 76*(4), 611–641.

Rogers, J. (2004). Creating a public accountability for California's schools. *Teachers College Record, 106*(11), 2171–2192.

Oakes, J., Rogers, J., & Lipton, M. (2006). *Learning power: Organizing for education and justice.*

References

Epstein, J. (1992). School and family partnerships. In M. Alkin (Ed.), Encyclopedia of educational research (6th ed., pp. 1139–1151). New York, NY: Macmillan.

Epstein, J. L. (2002). *School, family, and community partnerships: Your handbook for action.* (2nd ed.). Thousand Oaks, CA: Corwin.

National Network of Partnership Schools. (2006). *Six types of involvement: Keys to successful partnerships*

About Parent-U-Turn

Objectives and Programs

Parent-U-Turn informs and educates parents and community members on ways to improve student academic achievement.

- Parent Survival Guide: PUT members developed *The Parent Survival Guide*, a bilingual guide to empower parents with the information they need to advocate for their children in school and to go to college. Parents will use *The Parent Survival Guide* to create a strong, workable environment in schools where the parents feel welcomed and respected.
- Parent Curriculum Project Institute: Parent-U-Turn members participated in this UCLA Parent Project 13-week institute, which helped them make sense of curriculum, California standards, instruction, and assessment. Parents formulated an understanding of their role in school reform efforts by creating an action plan, focused on how organized parent leaders can influence the quality of achievement of all students.
- Day of Dialogue: PUT organized the first Day of Dialogue in Lynwood, where teachers and parents came together to discuss why and how schools use the standards in the classroom.
- Parent Curriculum Program: PUT members offer this 13-week program in which parents learn about curriculum in language arts, science, history, and mathematics and about state standards, assessment, technology in the classroom, and statistics of student achievement in America.

Parent-U-Turn educates parents by modeling student-centered learning, authentic assessment, and the inquiry process.

- Parents participate in workshops comparing school A (a traditional school symbolized by a fortress) and school B (a 21st-century school representing the values of a family-centered school environment with an open-door policy in which the family feels welcome and participates in all levels of discussion and decision making within the infrastructure of school).
- Parents are engaged in a student-centered model classroom environment in which they play the role of students. In this student-centered model, parents grapple with the meaning-making of school curriculum and constructing their own understanding of how learning is organized in the classroom. Parents use hands-on activities to solve problems and use critical thinking as a way to learn about alternative ways of learning.

Parent-U-Turn provides information to parents and students about college access:

- Los Angeles Basin Initiative Parent Conference (LABI): Parent-U-Turn organized, recruited, and facilitated this conference at UCLA, which was attended by over 380 parents. The focus of the conference was for parents to learn about college requirements, financial assistance, and how to work with the school counselor and administrators.
- College Preparatory Workshops: PUT members assisted the Early Academic Outreach Program department at UCLA in recruiting parents as facilitators. Parents participated in the application process by filling out college registration applications and financial aid packets.
- UCLA Latino Alumni Parent Conference: PUT members helped plan and implement this conference and recruited a total of 250 parents from the Lynwood Unified School to the UCLA campus. The purpose of the parent conference was to acquaint parents with university campus resources, the politics of bilingual education, strategies, and for language acquisition and financial resources for colleges.
- Furthermore, parents participated in an open forum with higher education representatives about college preparatory requirements as well as a principal/teacher panel about issues of public schooling.

Parent-U-Turn provides parent leaders with opportunities to analyze and reflect on how the issues of school restructuring, social justice, and multiculturalism will affect their school communities.

- UCLA Center X/IDEA online Journal: UCLA Center X and IDEA created an online journal that represents voices from teachers, students, and the community. After participating in workshops on the topic of "What Does Democracy Looks Like?" members reflected on their educational goals for their children as well as concerns about the community surrounding the schools. Parents participated in group discussions, writing compositions, and editing each others' work. Members' writing and pictures are presently published on the online journal at www.TeachingToChangeLA.org.

- Parents are provided an environment for them to analyze and reflect on how issues of school restructuring, social justice, and multiculturalism affect their school communities by providing comparative data about local and national schools' curriculum, teaching pedagogy, and school resources. Parents participated in group discussions and role-played to make sense of data and information.

Parent-U-Turn works to establish a corps of parent and community leaders who can participate in educational reform efforts through access to skill-building resources.

- Training for Workshop Facilitators and Presenters: PUT members conducted two 4-hour workshops about how to facilitate groups around a discussion. In addition, participants engaged in a discussion on how to present a topic in a workshop setting. Workshop training included items on how to engage parents in small and large group discussions, warm-up activities, putting packets of materials together, and debriefing activities. Participants in this workshop served as facilitators and presenters at parent conferences, parent project institutes, and school meetings.

- Parent Action Plan Follow-Up: PUT parents representing schools having K–12 grades participated in 16 follow-up sessions at different community sites in Lynwood, Inglewood, and South Gate to continue to build leadership skills for implementing action plans of parents who completed a parent project institute.

Parent-U-Turn members work to increase parent involvement in decision making, especially those who have been traditionally disconnected from the schools.

- Parent districtwide conference: Lynwood Unified District parents participated in two days of districtwide conferences that were facilitated by PUT members and held at the Lynwood School District office. Parents planned and presented at the conference with 300 parents in attendance. The focus of the conference was for parents to obtain decision-making and communication strategies needed to assist them in navigating their children through the school system toward preparing all students for college.
- Parents who participated in the parent program are presently serving in the majority of positions on school councils at the local site and at the school district level. They meet regularly with the superintendent and attend school board meetings. Parents hold open orientation meetings and purposely recruit African American and Vietnamese families who are presently unrepresented in parent programs.

Teaching Teachers

UCLA Teacher Education Program (TEP) Parent Workshops

- PUT members organized and recruited 48 parents from Lynwood to participate in a workshop with teachers in the TEP program at UCLA. The purpose of this workshop was to engage parents and teachers in small group discussions on how the parents and teachers can involve the family culture in the curriculum to improve literacy. Also, the concept of "funds of knowledge" was presented, followed by a discussion as to a strategy for incorporating the strength of the family as a component of literacy education in the curriculum.
- The Urban Parent-Teacher Education Collaborative (UPTEC) is a community-based model of teacher education that includes urban parents in a preservice teacher education program. It is a 3-part teacher education course developed and co-taught by Dr. Anthony Collatos and urban parent activist Ms. Mary Johnson of Parent-U-Turn. UPTEC is also a 5-year research project that seeks to understand how preservice teachers' engagement in the program influences their perceptions of urban schools and communities,

how they include parents and communities in their classrooms, and how their identities as urban educators are formed.

Parent-U-Turn participates actively in the communities where they work.

- Scholarships for South Gate Youth: PUT members have sponsored a total of six students for the last 2 to 4 year commitment. Every year we sponsor an additional three students. Each student that we sponsor gets a check for $400. PUT also gives a $100 Savings Bond to two middle school students, one for most improvement and one for high achievement.
- Annual Thanksgiving Turkey Distribution: PUT members have done this event since 1997. PUT distributed an average of 450 turkeys/groceries to needy families in South Gate. Also, in Lynwood, PUT distributed 75 turkeys/groceries to needy families.

Author

Mary Johnson

Hometown: Dover, Delaware

Mary Johnson is the mother of four: three sons and one daughter, Ronald Johnson, Earvin Johnson, L.C. Johnson, and Mya Johnson, respectively.

Area of Expertise: urban education, parent involvement; NCLB educational access and equity, parent and student rights, education reform, and parent education.

Biography

Mary Johnson, co-instructor of urban schooling at Pepperdine University GSEP, specializes in the influence of racial and cultural differences on teaching and learning, particularly in urban schools, and how these differences affect the way teachers, parents, and students interact. As an advocate, she strives to identify new methods for distributing information about school conditions to state and federal agencies, and continues to collaborate with educational researchers, school administrators, educators, community organizers, and advocates.

She is regularly cited as an expert on NCLB regarding parent education and parent and student rights. Johnson has been recognized or cited in several book publications such as *Learning Power* by Dr. Jeannie Oakes and Dr. John Rogers, and in the 2007 *Harvard Review* winter edition written by Dr. John Rogers. She has conducted multiple workshops and seminars, working with teachers, parents, and administrators at all levels to improve teaching and learning in multicultural settings.

The 21st Century Parent, pages 57–58
Copyright © 2012 by Information Age Publishing
All rights of reproduction in any form reserved.

57

Johnson is also ex-chairperson for the Parent Collaborative at Los Angeles Unified School District, and she is president of the advocacy organization, Parent-U-Turn. As chairperson of the Parent Collaborative, Johnson's background as an advocate has helped her lead the way to the transformation of LAUSD parent involvement from the 20th-century model to the 21st-century parent model, which sees parents as advocates and leaders. Johnson's interest is to create parent advocate leaders who help other parents navigate their children beyond high school into universities.

Contributing Editor

Valerie Munoz

mvadvocate2003@yahoo.com

Parent-U-Turn

Vice President

Ms. Munoz is Parent Liaison for the Lynwood Unified School District. Through the UCLA Parent Project at Center X, Ms. Munoz served as a parent director for the project. Since 2001, Ms. Munoz worked as a consultant or advisor for parent programs in various school districts such as Inglewood and the Los Angeles Unified School District. The program is a 13-week workshop series that empowers parents in how to navigate their children beyond high school and into a university.

As a parent educator, Ms. Munoz is able to help parents empower themselves to be the best advocates for their children and others. Ms. Munoz instills in parents the idea that knowledge is powerful for social change. She says, "We must know the history of education to prevent history from repeating itself."

As a Parent-U-Turn member, Ms. Munoz assisted the organization in coordinating the successful Day of Dialogue, in which teachers and parents came together to discuss state standards, and why and how the standards are used in the classroom.

CPSIA information can be obtained at www.ICGtesting.com
Printed in the USA
BVOW030623230812

298567BV00002B/1/P